STARTING AT THE TOP:

Learning the Nuances of Executive Leadership

Patrick G. Blanchard

ISBN-13: 978-1497300330
ISBN-10: 1497300339

Library of Congress Control Number: 2014905521

CreateSpace Independent Publishing Platform
North Charleston, SC

Typeset in Adobe Caslon
Cover Design and Layout: Kruhu

Cover image includes official portrait of author, Patrick G. Blanchard, at 27 years of age, while serving as Assistant State Treasurer of Georgia (1971).

TABLE OF CONTENTS

THE AUTHOR, PATRICK G. BLANCHARD, GIVING HIS ACCEPTANCE SPEECH AFTER BEING THE FIRST INDUCTEE INTO THE CSRA BUSINESS HALL OF FAME. (2003)

DEDICATION AND ACKNOWLEDGEMENTS

First, I dedicate this publication to my immediate family who taught me so very much, through their words and through their actions, about strong ethics, benevolence, and the importance of leadership. These family mentors included my grandfathers, Dr. Pierce Gordon Blanchard and the Honorable Jake (G. B.) Pollard, Sr., as well as my late father, John Pierce (J. P.) Blanchard, Sr.

Next, I dedicate this book to my mentors. My most significant mentors were entrepreneurs who created wealth and careers for the people within their professional spheres and then were also servant leaders in the volunteer arena of their communities. Many are quoted in these pages, while others I thank for the spirit of their guidance. This publication is further dedicated to all who lead us so effectively.

I also dedicate this book to my very good friend, Joe McGlamery of Statesboro, Georgia. Joe and Susan have always been very special friends to us and have been with us through all of the good times and challenges.

I appreciate the guidance toward the completion of this book by Dr. Constance Campbell, the W. E. Carter Distinguished Chair of Business Leadership at Georgia Southern University. Her assistance has enhanced the quality of this book.

Finally, and most importantly, I dedicate this book to my wife, Gwen, and my two children, Mary and Patrick, Jr., for their support of my business career and my volunteerism in every sense.

Patrick G. Blanchard
Augusta, Georgia
Winter 2014

FOREWORD

My first priority, upon becoming Dean of the College of Business Administration at Georgia Southern University in 1986, was to form a Business Advisory Council comprised of successful business men and women. In the process of seeking advice regarding potential members for this council from several regional business leaders, one name surfaced repeatedly: Mr. Patrick Blanchard, a Georgia Southern alumnus and a bank CEO in Augusta, Georgia. I realized very quickly that this was someone I wanted to meet.

Upon my first contact with him, not only did Mr. Blanchard enthusiastically accept this opportunity to serve his alma mater, he also agreed to serve as the council's chairman. As we became acquainted and began to work together, I quickly came to realize what the readers of this book will learn – Patrick Blanchard knows leadership. Over the ensuing years as we shared our commitment to Georgia Southern, we developed a special friendship and I have been privileged to learn many lessons from this remarkable leader.

Patrick's leadership experiences include CEO positions in three community banks that he organized, as well as two related holding companies across 36 successful and productive years. He has also served on more than 45 separate for-profit and non-profit boards, including 24 chairman or president positions thereon. His many successes in these roles underscore that he is highly qualified to author a leadership book.

Mr. Blanchard's professional successes have earned him substantial recognition as a highly-respected banking executive. In fact, America's most renowned bank consultant, Alex Sheshunoff, visited Patrick in Augusta in July of 1994 to discuss Patrick's visions of various banking theories. The Atlanta Business Chronicle repeatedly honored him as one of "Georgia's Top Performing CEOs" among all Georgia publicly traded companies, including a Top Five recognition during his last three years as President and CEO of Georgia-Carolina Bancshares, Inc.

Patrick's accomplishments as a volunteer for non-profit organizations are epic. He has devoted literally thousands of hours to economic development, historic preservation, the medical sciences, the military, and the arts. His service has been national, regional, and local in scope. He is credited for his leadership roles in fundraising campaigns that raised approximately $30 million in contributions.

Numerous organizations have honored Mr. Blanchard for his extensive record of professional and volunteer service. These honors include the National Career Service Award from Delta Sigma Pi, the professional business fraternity; honorary membership in Beta Gamma Sigma, the international business honor society; Hall of Fame inductions by Georgia Southern University and by Junior Achievement of the CSRA; designation as Brevet Colonel with Life Membership in Signal Brigade by the U.S. Army Signal Corps; an Alumnus of the Year Award from his alma mater; and recognition as one of "Augusta's Greatest Givers" and "Augusta's Most Influential Citizens." On May 30, 2008, Augusta's Mayor Deke Copenhaver proclaimed the date to be Patrick G. Blanchard Day in Augusta.

In this book Patrick Blanchard provides a common-sense approach on how to become a successful leader. He discusses the many leadership lessons he has learned across more than 50 years of inspired professional and volunteer experiences. His presentation is punctuated with relevant anecdotes involving interactions with those who guided him to success.

There are no tricks or gimmicks to Patrick's theories on leadership. Rather, the reader can take inspiration from Patrick's straightforward and sincere advice. In recent years I have been teaching a leadership course to MBA students. In my course I tell my students about Patrick's success as a leader, and I stress two lessons that I observed in his deportment. The first lesson is that you cannot be a success unless you have an abiding concern for those whom you are leading. I assure my students that you cannot fake caring. The second lesson is that to achieve success you have to be unfailingly unselfish. That's because good things happen to unselfish people. Patrick Blanchard epitomizes these two tenets and he makes them vividly apparent in this book. As he states at the end of his introduction, "Enjoy the learning"!

Carl Gooding, Ph.D.
Dean Emeritus
College of Business Administration
Georgia Southern University

CHAPTER I

INTRODUCTION

"You live a charmed life."

This was not part of the interview. I had already answered all of the young reporter's questions about the intense selection process I had endured to become a finalist for Ernst & Young's 2004 Entrepreneur of the Year Award, and she was gathering her material, preparing to leave. Her comment about my charmed life was a quick aside in the midst of her leave taking. A few minutes later, she was in her car, on her way back to Atlanta to file her report, yet her statement lingered in my mind and gave me pause.

Do I live a charmed life? I'm not so sure. There have been plenty of times when my life certainly did not seem very charm*ing*, but I can say with certainty that I have had a blessed life. Those who know me now might be surprised to learn that I was very quiet as a child, never having a vision of what I wanted to do in life, and never being overly ambitious. Most of what I have accomplished in life, I was invited to lead by someone else. Upon reflection, this has shown me that the influence of other people in each of our lives cannot be overstated. Furthermore, the importance of choosing the right people to influence our lives most certainly cannot be overstated.

My life is a case in point of the importance of building relationships with people of high character and capability. Upon graduating from college, I began my career in the Executive Training Program at the Georgia Railroad Bank & Trust, one of the finest, most ethical and properly-run institutions in banking. I had the very unusual experience of being invited to move to the Executive Suite after only one year in the Executive Training Program. The three years there marked the beginning of my real leadership training, where I wrote letters and speeches for the

CEO, Mr. Sherman Drawdy, on a daily basis and organized my first bank at the age of 26. Mr. Drawdy was known as one of the most highly-respected CEOs in banking, serving five times on the Administrative Committee of the American Banking Association and as a President of the Georgia Bankers Association. His philanthropic contributions were the basis for his many civic awards, including the first Citizenship Award ever presented by the Augusta [Georgia] Bar Association. Those of us who had the privilege of knowing Mr. Drawdy personally, though, remember him for his ability to interact respectfully with people at all levels of society, from the US Presidents he met to the poorest of the poor. I am pleased to be able to say that Mr. Drawdy was a tremendous mentor to me and one of the largest influences on my career.

With Mr. Drawdy's approval, I took a leave of absence from the bank to become perhaps the nation's youngest Assistant State Treasurer of the state of Georgia, at the age of 27. Due, in part, to the mentoring of people like Mr. Drawdy, I completed a successful three-year stint with the State before being invited, at the age of 30, to serve as the CEO of Georgia State Bank in Martinez, Georgia. This was the first bank that I organized.

Since that time, I have continued to serve in executive roles of banks for a span of over 34 years, remaining as CEO of Georgia State Bank for 11 years, selling the bank when I was 41, and subsequently serving as the principal founder of the Georgia Bank & Trust and its parent company, Southeastern Bank Corporation. In 1997 I was asked to manage the organization of a new bank, the First Bank of Georgia, and I served as the principal organizer of its parent, Georgia-Carolina Bancshares, Inc. Over that same period of time, I served in leadership positions in more than 40 organizations, both public and private, including a number of national and regional boards, as well as educational, local, private, and non-profit corporations.

I have worked diligently during my career, but my success would not have been possible without the assistance of numerous family members and mentors who gave me the gift of their wisdom and experience. I am fortunate to come from a family with a long history of leadership through service to others and to community. From my youth, I had countless opportunities to observe family members demonstrate leadership lessons in their actions and interactions with others, as well as in their attitudes about being in leadership for the benefit of the greater good. Again, Sherman Drawdy, mentioned above, is only one of the many individuals over the years who passed along to me deep insights about leadership through their words and their actions. My family background, my mentors and my life experiences in executive leadership positions all add up to a lifetime of study about executive leadership.

In addition to learning the lesson of the value of building relationships with quality mentors, another major life lesson I have learned through my experiences is that executive leadership is not simply about doing the same things lower and middle managers do, only with more people involved; rather, successful executive leadership requires a completely different mindset than that required for successful management at lower levels in organizations. I have had the frustrating experience of observing people who have high potential and seem like naturals for executive positions fail utterly when placed in the executive suite because they have been unable to adjust their mindset to a "big-picture" perspective. Many of these people had not had the opportunities to learn leadership from family members, mentors, and experience.

It is my strong belief that high potential individuals can learn how to adopt an executive mindset if they can become aware of what the executive mindset consists of and how to develop it. My purpose in writing this book, therefore, is to share with you the lessons about executive leadership that I have learned from my family, my mentors and my experience. Bookstores are already filled with books on the topic of leadership, but few of those books focus on the nuances that separate executive leaders from those who fail to reach the executive suite. Colleges of business and professional training programs that purport to help you develop your leadership skills abound, but, like the majority of books about leadership, these programs often focus on management thinking, not leadership thinking, and then only mid-level management thinking at that. Be assured that there is a world of difference between being a good manager and being a good executive leader. Executives focus on the "big picture" in the organization, developing missions and enacting a variety of styles of leadership, whereas managers, even at middle levels, primarily enforce policies and procedures.

John Adair, well-known expert on leadership and developer of the Action Centered Leadership approach, explains the distinction between leadership and management by comparing the etymology of the two words. The word leadership comes from an Anglo-Saxon word referring to the road ahead and implying decisions about the path to choose. The word management comes from a less ancient Latin word, *manus*, which means hand, and refers to handling machines or systems. Certainly, successful CEOs need both management and leadership skills, but management skills are relatively straightforward. Executive leadership, on the other hand, requires a complex combination of art and science, and a vision for the future.

This book will show you how to combine the art and science of leadership in order to be a successful executive in a for-profit organization. It will show you how to start at the top, not necessarily in an actual executive position, but how to start at the top with an executive mindset, picturing the company as yours and comporting yourself in that manner. We will start by exploring leadership from a broad, universal perspective and will then narrow our focus to exploring the profile of a successful executive leader. We will discuss a range of issues pertaining to executive leadership, from the *seemingly* minor issue of making a strong positive first impression, to the obviously major issue of helping others develop their executive leadership skills. As we consider each issue, we will discuss how you can develop yourself to match the profile of an executive leader. Along the way, I will use examples from my own experience to clarify and illustrate the points that are covered.

Some people may attempt to develop their executive leadership through the roles they undertake in the non-profit world, and you will see in later chapters that I believe strongly in contributing one's leadership expertise to the non-profit world. However, I believe that you should only offer yourself as a leader in the volunteer world after you have developed your executive leadership knowledge and skills by building an excellent record in a career. In the volunteer world, there are additional important lessons to learn in order to enhance your success in leadership positions, and those will be discussed in the following pages as well.

Whether you are a recent college graduate just starting on a career path that you hope will lead to the executive suite or you are a middle-level manager whose career has plateaued, this book will give you practical guidance about how to move forward. In brief, upon reading this book you will learn how to look like a leader, think like a leader, talk like a leader, and act like a leader – an executive leader! Enjoy the learning.

THE UNIVERSALITY OF LEADERSHIP

In many books about leadership, you will find at least a passing reference to the long tradition of leadership in human history. In some of these books, you will even find examples of leadership in ancient times. While this is laudable for its recognition of the leadership wisdom of the ages, it does not go far enough, for leadership is not an artifact of human invention; leadership originates in the natural code of behavior of life itself.

Genetic selection and the corresponding development of leadership traits among animals provide evidence for the universality of leadership, as well as he necessity of leadership for survival. Michael Korda notes in his book, *Power: How to Obtain It, How to Use It,* that virtually every class of mammals, birds, fish, and insects is tribal in nature. The foundation for tribal behavior is the ability to communicate and to organize, according to noted biologist Edward O. Wilson. Although the level of the animal kingdom's communication through signals may seem limited when judged by human standards, animals convey information through displays of behavioral patterns that have been specialized in the course of evolution. A major component of these displays, or forms of communication, is their utility in establishing a social order wherein one animal assumes a position of leadership. Various peculiarities in appearance and signaling among animals within a species serve as communications that identify the rank of individual animals within hierarchies of dominance. Animals in dominant positions in some primate societies, for example, use their social powers to terminate fighting among subordinates, surely a skill that is needed by business leaders today! If the dominant leader is removed, aggression sharply increases as the previously equally-ranked subordinates contend for the top position. Sound familiar?

A second example of leadership in animal societies reads almost as if it could be a description of today's office environment. The dominant elders in a wide range of the aggressively-organized mammalian species routinely exclude the young from the group, leaving the young to wander as solitary nomads or join bachelor herds. At most, the young are tolerated uneasily around the fringes of the group. Predictably, according to biologist Wilson, it is the young males who are the most enterprising, aggressive, and troublesome elements in the group. It is not only individual members of the animal group who jockey for dominance; members of the group may form separate bands and cliques that cooperate in reducing the power of the dominant male leaders. Another familiar trait.

Most animals, including nearly all vertebrates and a large number of advanced invertebrates, conduct their lives according to precise rules of land tenure, spacing, and dominance. These rules, notes Wilson, mediate the struggle for competitive superiority as enabling devices that elevate personal or group genetic fitness. Both Aristotle and Pliny noted the demarcation of territory and its defense by male birds, leading to newcomers being perceived as a threat to the status of all group members. As an example of this territorial defense, the sight of an alien bird energizes a flock of Canadian geese, evoking threat displays that are accompanied by repeated mass approaches and retreats. Anyone who is familiar with chickens will have observed the treatment accorded a new bird when it is introduced into an existing flock. Unless it is unusually vigorous, the new bird will be attacked for days on end by members of the flock and will be forced into the lowest status position of the flock. Sound familiar?

When zoologists speak of leadership, they are usually referring to the act of leading the group as it moves from one place to another. Fish that travel in schools, such as mullet and silversides, are "led" from moment to moment by whichever fish happens to be brought to the forward edge of the school of fish. Schooling fish generally choose as their leader the largest and most attractive fish; sounds like humans.

More highly evolved species display more advanced forms of leadership. For example, when members of a wolf pack travel in single file, any one of several individuals can take the lead, but during chases or threats, the dominant male assumes command. Once again, we can see the parallels between such behavior and leadership in today's organizational settings.

These examples illustrate that leadership among humans, widely considered to be the most highly-evolved species, is not so different from leadership among the animal kingdom, and we can conclude that leadership originated even before humans began to develop leadership systems. But it is also instructive, as we build our understanding of leadership, to consider how humans did develop leadership systems.

As the human species evolved from Homo Erectus nearly two million years ago into Homo Sapiens, "those with large brains," nearly 300,000 years ago and then into our own subspecies nearly 160,000 years ago, the complexity of human culture evolved as well, resulting in more complicated communications and the need for leadership as a force for survival. According to *Robert's Rules of Order*, the holding of assemblies of the elders, fighting men, or people of a tribe is a custom older than written history, however, we do have a number of recorded examples of leadership in ancient times.

As humans began to collect in civilizations where people worked at varied trades, formed governments, worshipped, and developed the ability to read and write, the need for leadership amplified. One of the earliest documented examples of leadership exists in records left by the Sumerians, a farming people who arose around 4,500 B.C. in lower Mesopotamia, an area known today as Iraq. Their written language, consisting of symbols that represent objects, was impressed into clay tablets creating what is, most likely, the first record of business transactions. In response to the inability of the people, as they congregated in larger and larger groups, to build water canals to support their agricultural work and to protect themselves from bandits in the desert, a chief emerged known as the "Big Man." The Big Man was advised by merchants and well-off landlords even as he supervised tax collectors, judges, and managers of canals. The early Sumerian maxim, "the poor do not have power," demonstrates the place of the poor in their society. Sounds like a contemporary maxim, doesn't it?

A thousand miles southwest of Sumer, another civilization was developing along the banks of the Nile, as Menes conquered and united Egypt around 3,000 B.C., making the northern town of Memphis his capital. Not long before the time of Menes, the Egyptians invented a writing system of their own, perhaps borrowing the idea of writing from the Sumerians with whom they traded. Certainly the Pharaohs of Egypt are examples of leadership success. In fact, the massive pyramids they constructed illustrate the Pharaohs' understanding of the value of symbols in leadership. These mighty tombs, visible from the Nile, reminded those who saw them of the ruler's might, and the building of those tombs likely endeared and bonded the pharaoh to the ruling class. Sound familiar?

The lengthy and well-documented Chinese culture offers yet another lesson on leadership in the ancient world. As the Egyptians were developing their civilization near the Nile in 3,000 B.C., the Chinese settled in the Huang He, or Yellow River, Valley of northern China, where they made pottery, made use of the wheel, built farms and made silk, but had not yet discovered writing or the use of metals. In the first documented era of Ancient China, the Shang Dynasty (1766-1122 B.C.), we see a highly developed hierarchical civilization, consisting of a king, nobles, commoners, and slaves. The Shang peoples, with their capital at Anyang in the northern Hunan province, may have traded with travelers from Mesopotamia and South Asia, from whom they learned agricultural methods, which they used to stimulate the growth of the ancient Chinese civilization. In addition to their agricultural practices, the Shang people were known for their use of jade, bronze, horse drawn chariots, ancestor worship, and highly organized armies.

Like other ancient peoples, the Chinese developed unique practices, among which was their form of writing, finalized by about 2,000 B.C.

and consisting of a complex system of picture writing, using forms called ideograms, pictograms, and phonograms. Oracle bones, on which they inscribed their writing, were used for fortune telling and record keeping, thereby leaving a record of their civilization for future generations and enlarging our understanding of ancient Chinese society.

The Chou dynasty (1122-221 B.C.) saw the full flowering of ancient civilization in China. As a result of leadership decisions, the empire during this time was unified, a middle class arose, and iron was introduced. Confucius (551-479 B.C.), the sage, lived during the Chou dynasty and wrote a code of ethics that dominated Chinese thought and culture and shaped its leadership for the next 25 centuries.

There are fewer remaining records of ancient societies in the European region than there are from places like Egypt and Asia, but we do know that the Germanic tribes had a system of leadership in which freemen came together to make "by-laws" for their village and administer justice. The Norman Conquest in 1066 brought England under tight military control by the French; however, the structure of the Anglo-Saxon government was left largely intact.

All of these examples demonstrate the influences of leaders and leadership skills in ancient times, both in the animal world and in humankind. Their similarity with our current experience leads us to ask whether humanity is much changed since those ancient times. Is present-day leadership simply a matter of inbred instincts? This is the topic we consider in the next chapter.

IF THE BUGLER DOESN'T SOUND A CLEAR CALL: "NATURAL" LEADERSHIP

The question of whether leadership is inborn or developed, nature or nurture, has been debated for centuries, but numerous centuries ago, I believe that Shakespeare answered that question with the most accurate statement about leadership that I have ever seen: "Be not afraid of greatness; some men are born great, some achieve greatness, and some have greatness thrust upon them." If we substitute the words "leaders" and "leadership" for the words "great" and "greatness," we have an inclusive description of the origins of human leadership. Surely we have all known, or known of, individuals whom we would classify as natural leaders, people for whom leadership seems to be second nature, rather than a conscious act. We have known others who, though they may not appear to be a "born" leader, set their sights upon a leadership position and work hard to develop the skills that will take them in that direction. And we have known still others who have been unwittingly cast into a leadership role due to circumstances beyond their control. In this chapter we will focus on the first category – those who are born leaders. In particular, we will consider the role of family background as a contributor to natural leadership, thereafter addressing the question of whether there is hope for those who aspire to leadership but lack a family background replete with leaders.

Saint Paul describes leadership as a spiritual gift, asking the question, "If the bugler doesn't sound a clear call, how will the soldiers know they are being called to battle?" At the time these words were written, the bugler's call was a signal to gather together, to unite for a common purpose, and to be energized for that purpose. Lacking a clear call, none of these goals could be accomplished. Being a bugler who sounds a clear call means being an individual who knows where he or she is headed, knows how to get there, and engages others in joining the journey. My late father, John

Pierce Blanchard, was described by longtime friend Frank Christian as a person who always knew exactly where he was going and who always had a host of people who wanted to follow him. My father was a bugler who gave a clear call, and I was fortunate to learn many leadership lessons from his life of service to others.

John Pierce Blanchard Sr. came from a family who had the advantage of both education and cultural literacy. He recognized the value of a good education early in life, as evidenced by his position as the 15 year-old valedictorian of the Leah High School class of 1936. The valedictory address that he authored and presented to his graduating high school class was a prescient indicator of the values that would define his life, as well as solid advice for us today. "I would advise you to take a good grip on the real joys of life," he suggested, "to play the game like an adult, to fight against nothing so hard as your own weakness." J.P., as he was known to his friends, believed that the real joys of life included taking advantage of the opportunity to work hard to develop one's abilities and learning how to profit from the inevitable difficulties along the way. "As you grow greater, your opportunities grow greater; they are waiting for your development. As you grow greater, your troubles will grow smaller; for you will see them through greater eyes and look down upon them from loftier peaks of vision. Each day becomes a greater, happier day, for our horizon of life widens as we rise." The goal, however, was not simply to rise to the top, for "getting to the top is the world's pet delusion. There is no top. Every top we reach is the bottom of the next ascension." Rather, the goal for him was the satisfaction of having done one's best by using one's efforts and abilities in service to others. "You should base your expectations of reward on a solid foundation of service rendered," he admonished. "You should be willing to pay the price of success in honest effort. You should look upon your work as an opportunity to be seized with joy and made the most of, and not as painful drudgery to be reluctantly endured." I would see these values of taking joy in life, seizing opportunities, developing one's abilities to the fullest, and using those abilities in service to others played out in his life over and over again.

"Joy" is a word we do not hear often, particularly with respect to work activities, but my father exhibited *joie de vivre* in all of his life activities. He lived a life of joy in his work. After working as the Assistant Supervisor of Education for the Civilian Conservation Corps in Blaine, Oregon, and upon completion of a Bachelor's degree at Georgia Southern University and later a Master's degree at the University of Georgia, J.P. returned to Appling, Georgia to be the principal at the same Leah High School where he gave the valedictory speech quoted above. He spent five years as a principal, coach and teacher at Leah High and one year as the Director of Academic Training for prisoners of war at Fort Gordon, Georgia. In 1948, at the age of 28, he was elected Superintendent of Schools for the Columbia County, Georgia school system, a position he was elected to without opposition for the next 32 years. He was active in numerous professional educational associations, including as a principle organizer of the County School Superintendents Association of Georgia. Working with school superintendents in three other Georgia Counties, he secured a cooperative educational agency for their region called the Little River Shared Services Education Agency, which later became the CSRA Cooperative Educational Service Agency. His life's work has been recognized with numerous accolades, some of which are brick and mortar, like the "John Pierce Blanchard Stadium" at the Evans Comprehensive High School and the "John Pierce Blanchard Library" at Harlem High School and the statue of him at Blanchard Park in the village of Appling, Georgia. Other accolades are less tangible, yet just as meaningful, like his honorary life membership in the Georgia School Superintendents Association.

J.P. had his hand in a number of other enterprises as well, including the Columbia Publishing Company, publisher of the area newspaper, and the Blanchard Company, which was engaged in real estate, insurance, and other enterprises. J.P. also served in leadership positions in a variety of non-profit organizations, spanning appointed positions in Georgia Government. Among other high-level appointments in state government, he was appointed by the Governor to a committee on revising all of the Georgia laws pertaining to juveniles. He provided leadership in the Boy Scouts, as well as his college alma mater, Georgia Southern University, and military causes. My father's participation and leadership in such a broad variety of organizations, vocational and avocational, demonstrated to me the value of broad-based experience, service to community, and just plain having fun.

Of even greater import than his specific leadership experiences is that my father's joy in life came from his understanding of the inherent value of people and his efforts to always reach out to them. His ability to connect to people through his excellence in oratory was well known, but, even more than his ability to eloquently voice the longings of people's hearts, he was known for his ability to listen. He often told me that people do not always know how to express their inmost concerns and they sometimes need time and space to talk just to get things out. This taught me the invaluable lesson of the value of respecting and paying attention to the people who make up any organization.

My father's *joie de vivre* was not only expressed through his career and the people he met because of it. On many occasions he allowed the fiddle he played in a bluegrass band to express his joy for him. He fished and hunted with enthusiasm, often using his camera to record his hunting and fishing trips and then publishing articles about his adventures. He worked to ensure that others could share in the joy of these pursuits by serving as President of the Columbia County Game and Fish Club and organizing wildlife clubs throughout his region in Georgia. J. P's strong interest in conservation was recognized with the 1960 Governor's Award as "Outstanding Georgian" in Wildlife Conservation.

Most people who knew him would be surprised to know that my father was actually an introvert, deep thinking and basically a quiet man. Many is the time that my father and I got in the car in Augusta, Georgia to drive to Atlanta and spoke virtually not one word to each other during the entire car ride, yet neither of us found this to be uncomfortable. Our silence was more companionable than awkward. In public, though, my father was very outgoing and lively, conversing easily and genially with others. Through this, I learned that even the most genial of leaders must make time for introspection, reflection, and simply being quiet.

Certainly, I have had good fortune to spend time with a man like my father, whose life was a living example of some of the most important qualities of an effective leader, but I fully recognizing that this advantage is not of my own making. Any of us who have had the benefit of leadership training from the cradle upward would do well to fully recognize that we have this benefit solely due to the circumstances of birth, not through personal merit. It is particularly unseemly to be vain and pretentious if you are in this position. While I am not suggesting that you deny your family connections in your path toward executive leadership or refuse the benefits that arise because of them, my strong advice is that you allow others to discuss the merits of your family background, rather than boasting about it yourself and appearing audacious and vain. Boasting about something over which you had no control is completely risible.

Benjamin Franklin once said, "Life successes are not in holding good cards, but in playing well those you hold." Franklin certainly did not have a noble family history on which to build his long and varied career successes, and yet build successes he did. Everyone has a unique background and life story. Your background and life story may not appear, on first glance, to have gifted you with advantages, but everyone who aspires to a position of executive leadership would do well to consider his or her life story and determine what it has done to make you the potential executive leader that you are today. I would encourage you to identify your life experiences and family background as they pertain to your unique and innate leadership abilities. It is only by identifying your personal leadership qualities that you can use them to build your path toward executive leadership. Those who are not born with family connections or natural leadership abilities can still aspire to an executive position; it just may take a little more work for you to get there. In the next chapter, we will begin to see just exactly what that work should involve.

LOOKING LIKE A LEADER: CREATING STRONG POSITIVE FIRST IMPRESSIONS

"There are traits you are born with. You can't develop intelligence. You can't develop morals through the law. I learned my value system at the foot of my grandmother's chair before the age of seven," but "there are [leader characteristics] we develop; strategic thinking for example." Former CEO of 3M, George Buckley's thoughts, as quoted here, are consistent with Shakespeare's idea that some leadership is inborn, while other leadership characteristics are developed. The fact that Buckley spearheaded the movement of the 3M Company from a ranking of 15th among companies who develop the best leaders to number one among these companies certainly gives credence to his ideas. In this chapter, we will consider habits that can be developed that will help you achieve greatness – or at least to achieve true executive leadership.

Let us begin at the beginning with how to make a strong positive first impression. Will Rogers' oft-quoted statement that, "You never get a second chance to make a first impression," aptly sums up the importance of the first impression you make on others. Newspaper columnist Marilyn vos Savant aptly details the extent of the first impression you make on others with her statement that, "We present ourselves by the way we dress, our makeup or facial hair, hairstyles, facial expressions, body language, and more." When you realize that the first impression you make upon others can either ease your way onto the path toward executive leadership or create a large stumbling block which will be difficult to surmount, you will understand how important it is to be conscious of, and careful about, the first impression you make on others.

Making a good first impression starts with showing up for the race – and getting there before the race begins. Woody Allen tells us that "80% of success in life is by showing up." When you show up for the race toward the executive suite, you want others to view you as a person of quality, to think of you as a five-star leader, not a one-star leader. A Four or Five star hotel or restaurant, the ultimate in luxury and sophistication, gives an immediate impression of elegance through its high degree of hospitality and attention to detail. The entire staff should be genuinely friendly and capable. A one-star property, with its no-frills accommodations, appeals to the budget-minded traveler. The one-star leader is a person with minimal leadership qualities, while a five-star leader is the ultimate in leadership.

When King John of England came to the throne, he began a concerted effort to improve the wines of England, making a trip in 1201 to visit the King of France at his palace in Fontainebleau. There King John and his entourage were graciously granted free run of the palace and the French king's wine cellars. As Danziger and Gillingham report in their book, *1215*, a French writer of the time captured the poor first impression made by King John and his people, saying that, "After [King John] had gone, the King of France and his people all had a good laugh at the way the people of the English king had drunk all of the poor wines and left all of the good ones [untouched]."

I often wonder how many successful businessmen and women truly understand the magnitude of the impact their timeliness and judgment has on the first impression of them and on their continued success. I also wonder how many businessmen and women understand the magnitude of the *negative impact* of their habitual tardiness. Leading and leadership is always timely. Being on time is a significant leadership trait, while being tardy is an example of the lack of leadership.

For many years, my father organized and chaired a charity fishing tournament where a number of celebrity guests and political leaders fished in competition with the ongoing champion of the tournament, Dr. Doyne Smith. One year a retired Georgia governor, who was scheduled to participate in the tournament, failed to arrive when it came time to begin the caravan to the lake. Nonetheless, my father exclaimed, "load 'em up boys, it's time to go." From the crowd, a voice shouted, "But, J.P., the governor has not arrived yet," to which my father replied, "Boys, screw the governor, he has a watch just like me. Load 'em up." Fortunately, the former governor did show up soon afterwards and was able to join the group and enjoy the fishing competition, but those of us who are not former governors would do best to show up on time.

Many people do not understand that arriving too early does not create a favorable first impression either. Early in my career in my duties at the Georgia State Capitol, someone who arrived more than 30 minutes in advance of a meeting created a new challenge for us, since we had to find someone from among our limited staff to entertain the visitor until the time of our appointment. After years of experience, my suggestion is that you arrive five minutes early for meetings and appointments so that you do not interrupt your host's other activities, but you are available if they are free a few minutes earlier than scheduled.

If being timely is the first step to making a strong positive first impression, dressing the part of an executive is the second step. Early in my career, I noticed that some of my male colleagues paired their business suits with dress shirts in pale pastel colors. Wondering whether this might be a good way to add variety and style to the standard business attire, I asked a successful retail clothing executive, Randolph L. Burnnette, if it is appropriate for a man who aspires to executive leadership to wear pastel dress shirts in colors like light yellow, light blue or light green. Randy's response? "You'll never make a mistake by wearing a white dress shirt." Since that day over 25 years ago, I have always worn dark-color suits, white shirts, and conservative ties in my weekday career routines. Shirts that are monogrammed in a color that coordinates with one's tie do add a little zest to this business "uniform." There are many published comments on the warmth and respectability of navy blue, white and burgundy, and a man can never go wrong with a navy blue suit, white dress shirt, and a conservative, perhaps burgundy, tie. For women aspiring to executive positions, the style of dress must also be professional and understated. Michael Korda's book, *Power: How to Get It, How to Use It*, addresses the issue of appropriate footwear for men, suggesting that lace-up shoes communicate seriousness, whereas loafers for men communicate a carefree nature lacking in the gravitas necessary for executive leadership. In all cases, the most important consideration is to dress appropriately for the occasion – to look like a leader.

Discerning what is appropriate for the occasion can be a challenge at times, though. "Business casual" can mean anything from nice jeans to simply opting out of wearing a tie. It can be confusing if someone is giving a black-tie event and states on the invitation that it is black tie optional, because this indicates two separate conflicting suggestions for appropriate dress. In the words of my friend, former maître-d', Greg Tom, when in doubt, it is better to slightly over-dress for an event than to under-dress. When your host or hostess is making a concerted effort to organize a high-quality event, you can complement him or her by dressing appropriately. Under-dressing could offend your host or hostess.

Clearly, it is important to make a strong positive and professional first impression on others if you wish to move into executive leadership. Timeliness and professional dress will build a good first impression of your business habits and appearance, but you still need to build a strong positive first impression of your business capabilities. Having a high level of cultural literacy will aid you in this endeavor. You won't continue far toward the executive suite if you look good but lack substance. Not only should you look like a leader, you should think and act like a leader. Comedian George Gobel's statement, "the world is a tuxedo, while I'm a pair of brown shoes," epitomizes the experience of being out of step with the world at large. Being *in* step means following proper business protocols, such as choosing appropriate topics for discussion and appropriate times to discuss them. It also means being aware of comments that should not be shared. In short, becoming an interesting person will give you an invaluable boost toward becoming a successful executive leader.

Business men and women must have a talent for identifying which of their trainees will become their future leaders, and must be able to distinguish between future leaders and non-leaders often at a moment's notice. Informal conversations, such as cocktail conversations, oftentimes reveal more about the quality and effectiveness of a potential leader than does a résumé. As a matter of practice, I have found that if a potential leader cannot pass the social conversation literacy test, there is little reason to review their résumé. Therefore, it is always appropriate to become culturally literate, as described in E. D. Hirsch's book of the same name. Cultural literacy is your possession of the basic information needed to understand common topics and allusions that are part of the dominant culture in today's world. For example, you should recognize the comment, "his speech was longer than The Ring Cycle," as a reference to Wagnerian opera. The most interesting leaders I have known are culturally literate in four primary areas; interesting personal experiences, associating with interesting people, traveling to interesting places, and reading interesting material.

You have seen that I was fortunate to have the privilege of growing up in a family of people who had interesting personal experiences to share. Early on, I was aware that our family was a literate and educated family, and I assumed that everyone should have an opportunity to earn a college education. My positive childhood learning experiences gave me a great appetite to become more literate and even to develop personal growth objectives for my own literacy prior to attending college. Therefore, it was an eye-opening experience for me, as a freshman at Georgia Southern University, when I first saw other students, often first-generation college students, who were highly capable of preparing for classroom examinations, but who were not culturally literate.

· Cultural literacy does not embrace the whole spectrum of education, according to Hirsch's work on cultural literacy, but neither is it limited to only an acquaintance with the arts. Cultural literacy spans a broad domain, extending across human activity from sports to science, and it is not the purview of only one social class. The subjects that fall under the heading of cultural literacy number as many as 5,000 individual separate points of knowledge, and 80 percent of these points of knowledge have a past history greater than 100 years. Hirsch decries the decline in American cultural literacy at exactly the point in time when our changed economy should require cultural literacy to be on the upswing. Some believe that our schools are at fault for this turn of events, but that even they may be powerless to change the endless cycle of poverty and its accompanying cultural illiteracy.

While it may be accurate that our literacy is declining, in my view, cultural literacy constitutes the only sure avenue of opportunity for disadvantaged children, young adults, and the old alike. Most individuals have the resources and the power to lift themselves out of ignorance and poverty by setting out to develop a specific learning program targeted, among other things, at building their cultural literacy. Individuals can break the cycle of poverty and ignorance only if they make a concerted and continued effort to move beyond their environment in a highly upward-bound fashion.

Indeed, developing cultural literacy is a must if you want to think like an executive leader. Hirsch points out that familiarity with the wide-ranging knowledge base that should be a hallmark of an educated person is largely lacking among young people now in their twenties and thirties and is an important contributor to the lack of cultural literacy that corporations, large and small, are now finding in their middle-level executives. This lack of a shared body of knowledge is a chief component of these individuals' inability to communicate effectively, thereby rendering them incapable of acting like an executive leader. Effective oral and written communication skills require a large body of shared background and knowledge.

Your life experiences may be vastly different, but everyone has a story to tell, and yours will be interesting too, if communicated appropriately. You can also build your store of experiences, experiences that go beyond career activities. Attending significant events of history, or perhaps attending significant presentations about such events, can be achieved on the most modest of budgets. Thus, one way to build cultural literacy is to pay attention to and build your own life story and learn how to communicate it in an interesting manner.

A second way to be interesting is to associate with interesting people. Include interesting social experiences in your quest to become an executive leader. Look for opportunities to attend high-quality, black-tie cocktail events where you can meet, study and listen to good conversation with business and community leaders.

There is much to learn simply by listening to and studying the style and mannerisms of quality leaders as previously stated. I had the unique opportunity to be associated with one of the finest bank CEO's in the history of Georgia banking, Mr. Sherman Drawdy. Mr. Drawdy was an influential mentor, not only to me, but to many others who also had the opportunity to come in contact with him in his role as CEO of the Georgia Railroad Bank & Trust Company. Although Mr. Drawdy was a relatively quiet man, his qualities as an executive leader were deep and far reaching. Unquestionably the captain of the ship, Mr. Drawdy built a culture at Georgia Railroad Bank for the highest of ethical standards, the best treatment of all people associated with the bank, and the clearest adherence to proper business protocol. When he passed on in 1973, I had already been affirmed as the CEO of Georgia State Bank and was well positioned in my career, however, I firmly believe that my future would not have been nearly as eventful had I not had the good fortune of being mentored by Mr. Sherman

Drawdy. He was the kind of person with whom we should all aspire to associate.

Not only have I had the good fortune to develop friendships with notable Georgians, but also with notable entertainers and other impressive personalities. I had the experience of playing golf in a pro-am foursome and sharing an afternoon with the international economist and television newscaster, Lou Dobbs. Our two other partners were the true golfers among the foursome, and they actually won the tournament for us, but it was quite a thrill when the winners of the Pro-Am tournament were announced at that evenings awards dinner as Blanchard and Dobbs! Dobbs made me look good at a later time when he described our victory and friendship to a Metro-Augusta Chamber of Commerce gathering at a gate of the Reagan National Airport. Take advantage of any opportunity you have to visit with people of renowned reputation.

A third way to become an interesting person is by visiting interesting and unique places, including renowned restaurants, museums, and by attending major sporting events like the Masters Tournament, the Kentucky Derby, the All-Star and World Series baseball games, and the Super Bowl. These experiences strengthen your public image and provide you material to participate in interesting convivial conversations. Traveling to interesting places can be achieved without great expense, and it is important to attend world-class events even if your budget is limited, because they broaden your perspective. Major cities will have museums and theatre venues, like the High Museum of Art and the Fox Theatre in Atlanta, where you can be introduced to high-quality arts of various quality presentations.

If your schedule or finances prevent you from traveling widely, spending time reading will increase your knowledge of noteworthy issues, places, and events. One of my mentors, Dr. Alex Murphey, once said the most valuable possession he had growing up was a library card, which allowed him access to literally thousands of books, putting all of the world's history and culture at his fingertips and ultimately leading him to a successful career in medicine. According to E. D. Hirsch, reading and writing are cumulative skills; the more we read, the more baseline knowledge we gain for further reading. Even if the pursuit of cultural literacy is not undertaken in the early years, it is never too late to start. Virtually all leaders develop a strong habit of reading, making it a daily exercise. Among all of my CEO friends, we share a joy in the hobbies of travel, art, music, food and beverage, and reading good books. Most of our gifts to each other are good books or vintage beverages.

Make it a goal, therefore, to read widely and wisely through public libraries, discount book stores, the Internet, and developing your own personal library of good books. Good reading of the classics and contemporary writings enhances your knowledge and opportunities as a potential leader. Subscribe to quality publications, such as the *Wall Street Journal, Forbes* magazine, and *The New Yorker* magazine to build your knowledge of world affairs. Join the Musical Heritage Society, the Jazz Heritage Society and high-quality book, CD and DVD clubs. There are myriad essential names, phrases, and concepts that every leader needs to know. A sampling of such items, ranging from A-Z includes: Acropolis, John Adams, Aesthetics, Alzheimer's disease, Amazon, Beijing, Enrico Caruso, *C'est la vie,* DNA, Miles Davis, GOP, Grinch, Ides of March, Diana Krall, Eva Peron, Rosh Hashanah, 1066, 1492, 1861-1865, 1939-1945, and Zen.

Some people, such as Dr. Mark Bauerlain, author of *The Dumbest Generation,* argue that the intellectual future of the United States looks dim, not in terms of economics, technology, medicine or media, but in terms of civil understanding and a liberal education. This suggests a pressing need to place cultural literacy high on the list of our educational priorities, even at the preschool level. Bauerlain decries the apathy among the young generation of today toward history, civic principles, foreign affairs, comparative religions, serious media and art. Hirsch includes science as an additional subject of importance as a noble achievement and a great expression of the human spirit. I truly believe that liberal arts learning and knowledge of the world we live in, or lack thereof, can make or break a potential executive leader or CEO.

I have seen an example of this experience when attending Founder's Day events at the Alpha Tau Omega (ATO) fraternity chapter that we founded and presided over 50 years ago at Georgia Southern University. The young men and women I meet today during the annual Founder's Day events are typically well mannered, well dressed, well-appointed young men and women with special people skills and clear leadership talent. This reassures me that there are young people today who are culturally literate and who will carry us toward a positive future.

The value of participating in a social organization, like a fraternity, and the importance of taking on leadership responsibilities early in life are two lessons that were brought home to me in the mid-1990s when I attended the National Legislative meetings of the Independent Bankers of America in Washington, DC. At a formal breakfast during the meetings, I was seated with four other CEOs of bank holding companies, all of us around 40 years of age. In addition to our common ages and positions, we also discovered that each of us had been president of our social fraternities during college. It is not surprising that leadership experiences in college were predictive of leadership experiences later in the business world.

The great French politician and gourmet cook, Anthelime Brillat-Savarin, once said, "Tell me what you eat, and I will tell you what you are." In this section, I have argued that not only what you eat, but what you drink, the material you read, the topics of your conversation, the music you listen to, the style of art you have in your collection, and the places you visit in person or through reading all tell us who you are. By seeking out these experiences for yourself, you will become a more natural leader.

First impressions can either be a great asset on your path to executive leadership or they can be a stumbling block which is only overcome with great difficulty. In this chapter, we have considered ways to make a positive first impression through your appearance, your conversation and through enlarging and broadening your life experiences. Strong leaders make a positive first impression with their appropriate appearance, they can engage in good conversation, they have knowledge of American history and world events and are culturally literate, interesting and informed. People such as these are primed for executive leadership success, because they look like a leader and talk like a leader. But we move into deeper waters when we consider how to think like a leader. We'll wade into the water on that topic in the next chapter.

THINKING LIKE A LEADER: INTELLIGENCE AND ETHICS

There is an individual characteristic that is so important for executive leadership that it is deserving of its own standalone discussion; being able to think like a leader. There is wide agreement that we are all born with a range of intelligence, above or below which we cannot go, but that the exact point within that range at which our intelligence settles is somewhat mutable and malleable. Intelligence is a key component of thinking like a leader, so in this chapter, we shall consider the varieties of intelligence and the interaction between intelligence and learning.

Even during the very early preschool period of my life, I enjoyed sitting in family groups and listening to adult conversation. Although I certainly would not have described it in these words at that time, what I observed in these conversations was a combination of logic, philosophical wisdom and relatively strong scientific understanding. This early exposure to objective thinking enabled me, early on, to discern when others in our small village of Appling, Georgia made judgments more subjectively on the basis of superstition, incomplete thoughts and incomplete knowledge. It seemed odd to me, even at the time, that my experiences with learned adults enabled me to see issues more clearly than even some senior adults I met. My late father often told my brothers and me that, "just because someone is smart does not mean that they are always right in their decisions, but it does tell you where to bet your money."

Having been fortunate to be involved in enriching experiences early in life, I developed a hunger for knowledge and experience. Consequently, as I progressed through elementary, middle and high school, I sought understanding of literature, poetry, philosophy, general culture and music, all of which only made me more intensely interested in continuing to develop cultural literacy throughout adulthood. As we have discussed already, even without the benefit of enriching experiences early in life, it is still possible and important to develop cultural literacy as an adult who aspires to executive leadership positions.

Upon entering college, I had an eye-opening experience that taught me the importance of being intelligent and of appreciating and surrounding oneself with very bright individuals. This was my first time to encounter, among a few of the very gifted professors and the most exceptional students in classes with me, individuals whose Intelligence Quotient (IQ) appeared to be 160 and above. Admittedly, many of these individuals did not demonstrate strong interpersonal skills or high cultural literacy, but I learned very quickly that it was a good idea to identify the smartest student in each difficult class and become a study partner with them!

Interestingly, the early historic study of IQ was initiated when the French government commissioned psychologist Alfred Binet to create a testing system to differentiate normal children from those who were "inferior." Through the years, testing of IQ has been updated in attempts to design a test that is fair to all and where the average score falls at 100 and the scores are distributed such that they form a bell-shaped curve when plotted. As the diagram below indicates, a score of 100 would form the middle and the highest point on the bell because the greatest numbers of test-takers score at this level. Scores slightly above and below

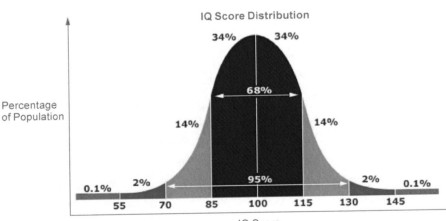

100 would also be common, though slightly less common than would the mean score of 100. As IQ test scores deviate further above and below 100, fewer individuals would score in those ranges, resulting in a plot of scores that, as an example, curves downward as the scores deviate further from 100.

When I was invited to take on an assignment in the executive suite and leave the Executive Training Program at Georgia Railroad Bank & Trust Company, 18 months after I had joined it, I had my first opportunity to observe intelligence in action on the job. In the course of performing my new job responsibilities, I was often in meetings with the executives of our bank, as well as executives at other corporations, and it was here that I truly began to understand the qualitative differences among various levels of intelligence. Four years later, in the summer of 1970, there were speculations that I would be named to an important position in Governor Jimmy Carter's new administration. In the process of interacting with other potential administration members, I had the opportunity to see an amazingly wide range of IQ levels, ranging from very low levels to clear levels of brilliance.

At about age 32, as I was in my first bank presidency, I had an experience that illustrated to me the value of learning and intelligence. One morning I was called to a construction site by the general contractor and architect on a building project. Actually, "summoned" would probably be a more accurate description of their request for me to visit the construction site. The general contractor explained that they wanted to discuss the size of the water pipes to the bathrooms in the building. The plans called for a one-half inch water line to the bathroom, but the contractor told me that they could triple the water supply to the bathrooms by installing a one-inch pipe instead, at no additional cost. Realizing that my approval of the larger pipe could either be a great success or the corporate equivalent of a snipe hunt, I knew that I must consider the options carefully. As the two older individuals stood waiting for my decision, I knew that I did not have the luxury of time. Upon quick consideration, it may not seem reasonable that replacing a one-half inch water line with a one-inch water line could possibly triple the water supply. But that's where the importance of learning came into play, as I remembered learning about the mathematical constant of the ratio expressed by the symbol Π (pi) and could quickly picture the effect of the expansion of a circle from one-half to one inch. After confirming with the contractor that this increase in the size of the pipe would not result in any increase in cost, I approved the one-inch water line.

As I returned to my automobile to leave the site, an elderly man old enough to be my grandfather followed me. I *think* his motives were pure and that he was trying to be helpful when he said, "Mr. Blanchard, those two men just lied to you. Any fool knows that you can't increase a water line from one-half inch to one inch and triple the water supply." This experience reminded me that not everyone has had the opportunity of formal education and that those who are fortunate to have the opportunity should realize their good fortune and take full advantage of their opportunities to develop higher-level thinking skills that are firmly grounded in knowledge and science.

My experience tells me that the bell-curved shape of the plot of IQ scores is a bit misleading, though, because the curve implies that differences in IQ scores are linear and additive, when in reality, they are more a matter of logarithmic differences. In other words, individuals who have an IQ of 160 are not simply 60 points higher than a person with an IQ of 100, but are far beyond the average score of 100. A leader with an IQ of 145 points is not a mere 45 points above the norm; he or she may be 100 times smarter than the norm! This point was further validated in 1997 when, as part of my duties as Chairman of the Augusta Metro Chamber of Commerce, I had dinner with Marilyn Vos Savant, noted columnist and lecturer, known for having the Guinness World Record for the highest recorded IQ of 190. Under other measurement systems, her IQ had been measured to be as high as 228. My conversations with her at dinner were world-class and delightful, once again illustrating the importance of understanding IQ. Quite simply, smarter people tend to make smarter decisions.

Be aware that your intelligence level is a trait you are born with, quite different from many other leadership skills, but one of the advantages of being in an executive leadership position is that you do not have to have an IQ of 160 yourself in order to be successful; rather you should learn to identify those who do have soaring IQs and not be afraid to surround yourself with them. Over the years I have learned to evaluate the intelligence capacity of those with whom I have relationships and have determined that I am most comfortable with those whose IQ scores of 135 to 144 place them at the threshold of genius. These people were typically CEOs and community leaders.

One of the challenges of executive leadership is finding a valid way to evaluate the intelligence level of potential executive-level leaders. One of my mentors and an expert in human resource issues, Bill Hatcher, Sr., attacked this challenge by putting together a multifaceted process for identifying executive leadership talent that involved, among other things, the use of three valid and reliable self assessments, the Wonderlic Cognitive Ability Test, the Kuder Career Interests Assessment, and the Predictive Index.

The Wonderlic Cognitive Ability test, formerly the Wonderlic Personnel Assessment, is a measure of intellect that also assesses aptitude for learning a job and solving problems. Because of the complex issues and problems that inevitably arise when managing an organization, it is imperative that we hire executive leaders in whose judgment we can have complete confidence. When we hire a person for an executive leadership position, we are hiring for today's challenges, but we are also hiring for the larger, more complex organization that will exist as the company grows. We want to hire an individual whose cognitive abilities not only enable them to lead in the organization as it currently exists, but are also broad and deep enough to successfully grow with the organization and manage future complexity. Before using the Wonderlic myself as part of the hiring process, I recall hiring individuals whom I believed to be highly capable, only to discover that they were neither capable of taking complex instructions nor of resolving complex problems. We want to avoid the dysfunction that occurs when company activities outgrow the management team, and the Wonderlic is a way to make that less likely to happen!

The second assessment that measures leadership potential is the Kuder Career Interests Assessment, which explores avocational as well as vocational interests and matches them with appropriate career paths, helping increase job satisfaction by matching the applicants' interests with their jobs. For example, the assessment indicates whether an applicant would rather read a book or go fishing. When managing a diverse group of managers, it is extremely important to understand the natural preferences of your leaders and use the information for your and their best advantage and for bonding.

The most important of the three assessments to use for hiring executive leaders is the Predictive Index Assessment, which clearly indicates whether the applicant has true leadership capabilities. This assessment can be used to determine the applicant's personal and professional interests and to indicate the applicant's confidence, team orientation, performance drives, management styles, capabilities, potential interests and motivation. The Index measures your drive to exert your influence over people and events. It further measures the drive for social interaction with other people and your drive to conform to formal rules and structures. The Index also measures the extent to which one is either subjective or objective with respect to judgment and decision making. In my experience of selecting candidates for executive positions, I have observed a large divide between those who seek to base their decision making on objective information and those whose regular thinking is hampered by an abundance of unrecognized prejudice.

To give you an idea of the information provided in the results of the P. I. assessment, here is an excerpt from the P. I. results for one of our executive leadership team members:

> His work pace is faster-than-average. He is able to learn quickly, thoroughly, and in detail, and will recognize and adjust to change once well-informed of the need for it. While he is impatient with repetitive handling of routine details, [this individual] is a self-disciplined person who can do a good deal of that kind of work as long as it is only an intermittent aspect of his job, and not his primary responsibility.

A very useful additional component of the results from this assessment is the management strategies that are recommended as a good match with the personal characteristics of the test taker. For example, for the candidate above, the results indicated that this person should be provided with: "As much independence and flexibility in his activities as possible," and "Opportunities to prove himself, and recognition and reward for doing so." This kind of feedback would be very helpful for you to have about yourself, so that you can more closely align your innate abilities and personality with appropriate leadership positions.

I have taken the Predictive Index myself and have often used it as part of our executive hiring process. Interestingly, our succession plan at First Bank was that Remer Brinson, a young man who appeared to be a "natural" as a banker, would follow me as CEO of the company and the bank. Upon comparing our Predictive Index scores, we found them to be very similar, which suggests to me a compatibility in our management styles which will engender continuity at the bank as he has moved into executive leadership positions. We laughed as we noticed that our P. I.'s both indicate that we are rule players. What a natural trait for a career in banking! Remer and I also have similar family backgrounds where we had the opportunity to learn much about leadership through family observation. This gives us the ability to use a flexible approach to decision making and solving problems when appropriate. The similarities in our profiles on the P. I. confirmed my belief that, of all of the recruitment tools we used, the Predictive Index is the assessment of greatest value for identifying executive leaders.

In addition to self-assessments as a way to evaluate leadership potential, Mr. Hatcher also recommended gaining a full picture of leadership applicants' character, looking especially for individuals of high character and strong ethics. Although it may sound trite, you will want to be sure that a criminal background check on you would come up spotless. I recommend performing a criminal background check on all applicants, looking for felonies or misdemeanors, including a police report. Sometimes business leaders are surprised when they find that an otherwise appealing *bona fide* applicant has had legal or ethical problems in the past.

In addition, the application process should include a credit check on the applicant. Even though this may require written approval from the applicant, you must know that your potential executive has a high credit rating with no blemishes on their credit standing. A good credit rating reflects good personal behavior and strong integrity. Clearly, hiring a future executive with a criminal background or poor credit rating sets you up for disaster. Finally, consider what an individual's lifestyle reveals about their character. Lifestyle issues can be observed by looking at lifestyle practices and hobbies. While these practices and hobbies, particularly expensive ones, can be merely a form of entertainment, there is also the potential that they can run to excess and even sickness. Such sicknesses include gambling, alcoholism, substance addiction, and verbal abuse of others.

Lt. General Douglas Buchholz, the former Commander of the US Army Signal Corps at Fort Gordon, was a stellar example of an intelligent and ethical leader. Although I had been acquainted with him when he was the Deputy Commander of Fort Gordon, my first in-depth personal experience with the General was immediately after he was elevated to the position of Post Commander. Buchholz's first words to me, in my role as Chairman of the Military Affairs Committee of the Metro Augusta Chamber of Commerce, were, "Patrick, there's nothing you can do for me, but I will be watching to see how you good ole boys treat our soldiers." I knew right away that Buchholz was a man who *was not* looking for handouts from the community and *was* looking out for the good of the people in his charge, and I respected him for it. This was the beginning of a new commitment of the Metro Augusta Chamber and the community to strengthening its relationship with Fort Gordon, and Doug Buchholz single-handedly made it happen. Regretfully, he passed away at the early age of 57, due to leukemia, but as I prepared the special eulogy I had been invited to offer during his funeral, I realized that his legacy of intelligent and ethical leadership would far outlive his time on earth. In preparing my eulogy for Doug, I stated that, "Doug Buchholz was exactly what he appeared to be; he was the sum of great intelligence and a great sense of ethics."

We do not always see intelligence combined with ethics in the modern business world, but it is a combination of traits worth pursuing. During the 13th Century the colleges and universities in France and England taught ethics as a topic under the category of critical thinking, in recognition of the intelligence that is needed to fully understand the complex nature of ethics. A high standard of ethics is an absolute necessity for building a solid reputation, and a good reputation is an asset worth guarding at all costs. My distant cousin, Tommy Blanchard, who is a well-known business person in Augusta, stated it well. "Never lose sight of the fact that a good reputation is the hardest thing to earn and certainly the easiest thing to lose that you will ever have," he said, "so work hard and treat people fairly and things will work out all right." These recommendations were offered by Tommy Blanchard as he was inducted into the CSRA Business Hall of Fame in 2013.

Judge J. Randal Hall is a modern-day example of the combination of high intelligence and strong ethics. Judge Hall served as general counsel for our parent company and our bank, and assisted in organizing the First Bank of Georgia and Georgia-Carolina Bancshares, Inc. before being appointed a Federal Judge. Whenever Judge Hall provided us with a legal opinion, it was always clear and straightforward and coupled with an appropriate statement on the ethics of the issue.

One of my most interesting acquaintances provides another example of the combination of intelligence and ethics, singer/songwriter Larry Jon Wilson, who wrote and recorded some of the best lyrics and tunes to come out of Nashville in his time. Noted by Fred Foster, well-known record producer and owner of Monumental Records, as one of the most talented artists he had observed, Larry was also an excellent athlete with an extremely high level of intelligence who enjoyed reading and discussing intellectual issues.

On the topic of business ethics, he admitted to being a cynic, viewing "business ethics" as a prime example of an oxymoron. During our regular Saturday morning breakfasts together discussing a long list of issues, he enjoyed discussing ethics and religion. He would often ask how I felt "about the town crooks cheating their friends, neighbors and relatives Monday through Saturday and then spending time passing out programs and taking up collections along with the faithful members during Sunday morning church services," as witnessed by television broadcasts. I would admit that I shared his concerns and considered that this must certainly be confusing to even those who were fragile, but devoted Christians. We discussed the idea presented to me by a highly-admired Protestant minister that stated that these "town crooks" embraced a form of mental illness in their belief that they could practice unethical and un-Christian behavior for six days but be a committed Christian on Sundays. Although Larry Jon's and my careers were vastly different, our common pleasure in reading and discussing intellectual material and our shared commitment to ethical thinking brought Larry Jon Wilson and I together.

Regardless of your IQ score, you can build your store of knowledge and your ethical standards by earning a useful college degree. While you are completing your degree, you will have the opportunity to more fully identify your natural abilities and combine them with newly-acquired learning and skills in your chosen field. Appropriate degrees from colleges of business include accounting, economics, finance and marketing. Business students should also have a depth of knowledge about management theories. I do not recommend pursuing an undergraduate degree in management, since from a practical matter, most business executives earn their spot in the executive suite, in part, on the basis of their early success in one of the functional areas of business; finance, accounting, marketing or sales. Building credibility by experiencing *bona fide* success in your chosen area of business is a must before moving into an executive position.

Indeed, as we have seen, some of you will have the unearned advantage of family background and natural talents to assist you as you move toward executive leadership, but those who do not have those advantages need not despair, since there are many other ways to strengthen your executive potential by building your cultural literacy, advancing your ethical standards, and surrounding yourself with intelligent and ethical individuals. Everyone who aspires to executive leadership, whether you are a born leader, you achieve leadership, or you have it thrust upon you, will inevitably face struggles as you move toward the top of the organization. A wise leader learns to expect setbacks and know how to deal with them, as we will see in the next chapter.

POTPOURRI OF LEADERSHIP MEMORIES

His Royal Highness Prince Andrew of Great Britain,
Congressman D. Douglas Barnard, Jr. and the author

Ken Guenther, Patrick G. Blanchard and
Former Federal Reserve Chairman Alan Greenspan

FORMER UNITED STATES SENATOR MAX CLELAND AND THE AUTHOR

FORMER GOVERNOR OF GEORGIA CARL E. SANDERS AND THE AUTHOR

RENOWNED BANK CONSULTANT, ALEX SHESHUNOFF WITH THE AUTHOR

RENOWNED MANAGEMENT CONSULTANT AND AUTHOR, KEN
BLANCHARD, AND PATRICK G. BLANCHARD

S. Truett Cathy with the author

Best friends in food, beverages, and song: Larry Jon Wilson, Ron Harrison, Jim Beck, and Patrick G. Blanchard

CHAPTER 6

ACTING LIKE A LEADER: BUILDING YOUR COURAGE IN THE FACE OF STRUGGLES

No matter who your family may be; no matter how many interesting life experiences you've had; and no matter how polished you are, you will inevitably face struggles on your way to the executive suite. To navigate these struggles effectively, you must call forth courage and resilience. One of my lifetime mentors, Olin Plunkett, once explained that he liked my courage. As he described it, "You are not afraid." Displaying courage does not necessarily mean that you are not afraid; rather, courage may mean that you are willing to do what is right, even after you *are* afraid. Courage provides the intestinal fortitude to withstand all adversity and the resilience to react, respond, and recover on the way to accomplishment, achievement and victory. Other leaders admire leaders who have courage. The road to success is not a smooth path; therefore, you will have plenty of opportunities to build the courage of your convictions. In this chapter, we discuss some of the stumbling blocks that are commonly-experienced on the path to executive leadership.

The first step on the path to executive leadership is to chart your path. Develop a personal plan to reach your goal, with specific steps and timelines, and be prepared to take baby steps, if needed, in order to fulfill your plan. All of your decisions can then be weighed in light of their contributions to the achievement of your plan. On a day-to-day level, this may involve sacrifices in your personal life. When I was a young trainee, I witnessed many times when other trainees took themselves out of consideration for advancement because they were not willing to sacrifice their personal time or energy for the needs of the organization. As they would say, they would rather play golf.

One of my early mentors, Barney Whitaker, suggested that I consider every new career and volunteer opportunity in light of its long-term placement in my résumé. We have discussed the limitations in middle-management thinking, bound up as it is in policies and procedures, rather than "big-picture" thinking. In your pursuit to grow and learn, you must have the courage to begin a diplomatic process of shifting your thinking around the prejudices of society and of others who may view your thinking as skewed because they suffer from what I call middle-management thinking.

As you chart your path toward executive leadership, it is best to keep your ambitions to yourself, since there are those who may compete with you for those positions, even by emulating your best thinking or your personal plans. Initiate your move through the organization or industry without disturbing the natural day-to-day culture of the players. If you appear to be overly ambitious, there are those who will attempt to keep you in your place.

There are other challenges to your upward mobility. One is the limitations of time and another is the burden of responsibility. Early in my career, when given a large assignment with little time to complete it, I learned the value of awakening early, around 4am, to conduct my research and preparation of reports and speeches in order to remain on schedule. I remember early morning commitments at the State Capital when I served as Assistant State Treasurer. Busy hours in the office some days would lead to a civic club speech at lunch in one of our drive-to cities, such as Columbus, Georgia. During my drive, I would practice some of the lines in my speech and begin the process of recalling the names and faces of the community leaders in the approaching city where I was to speak. Often, I would know the area mayors, bank executives, and other business leaders personally and was expected to call them by name from memory. The importance of remembering names cannot be overstated and is a skill which should be acquired for all who aspire to a leadership role.

After my speech, there was a need to hurry back to Atlanta for daily appropriation approvals, our letter signing period, and then beginning the afternoon and evening rituals of 5pm cocktail receptions, dinners sponsored by professional organizations, and then having late evening drinks with older members of the General Assembly. The next day the same schedule would be repeated. It was during those days that I decided, if and when I became president of my own bank, I would follow a 7am to 7pm work schedule Monday through Friday and take soft matters, like informal friendly letter writing home for a few hours on both Saturday and Sunday. This practice is another strategy for out-performing the competition.

Veteran senior lender of Georgia Railroad Bank & Trust Co., Felton Dunaway, served as the Chairman of my Board during my first two years as CEO of Georgia State Bank. Mr. Dunaway had enjoyed a long-term career as a commercial lender, and he seemed to enjoy passing on his own pearls of wisdom to others like me. While regaling Mr. Dunaway with one of the major frustrations I experienced as a bank CEO, Mr. Dunaway gave me a word of advice, "Pat, I'm not worried about you and crooks; you will know crooks when you see them. But I am worried about your frustrations when you deal with those who talk a good game but can't quite deliver."

I now understand the accuracy of Mr. Dunaway's remarks, based upon reviewing approximately 36,000 commercial loan requests over my 34-plus years as a bank CEO. About 15% of those loan requests were easy decisions because they were submitted by the right borrowers with the right business plan—prompt approval was forthcoming. About 35% of the requests were easy decisions because they were submitted by the wrong borrowers with the wrong business plan—prompt rejection was forthcoming. The remaining 50% of requests were a struggle, because they were less clear cut—longer deliberations ensued, and sometimes our decisions resulted in thoughtful modifications.

Leaders prove they lack courage when they avoid conflicts. One of my favorite friends whom I meet regularly for conversations often discusses the energy and time used by those who try to rid themselves of conflict by avoiding it, but end up simply delaying the inevitable confrontations. One of my earlier officer assistants, Marc Wilson, Sr., would often remind me that conflicts do not resolve themselves and that the problems do not go away by ignoring them. Timing the resolution of conflicts is an important consideration. Sometimes delaying a discussion or possible confrontation can disturb the normal tempo of an organization. There are occasions when timing is everything in resolving conflicts. In dynamic organizations, confrontation can not only lead to resolving the issue but can even lead to more positive discussions and other positive decisions in time. And, there is the objective of honesty to consider. Avoiding conflicts or discussions is related to the honesty and integrity of the organization, because resolving conflicts quickly and effectively keeps the honesty and integrity in place. In sum, if you are to sit at the table of respected leaders, you must have the courage to become a master of resolving conflicts.

Becoming a master leader cannot be short-circuited by substituting cunning for knowledge and skill. A leadership challenge that is the ultimate in frustration occurs when listening to individuals who think they can outsmart the professional CEO. I have seen this scene played out over and over again on, literally, thousands of occasions. Put yourself in the place of the bank CEO, as a potential borrower leans his or her head in the office door, grins broadly, and asks, "Got a few minutes for me?" "Why sure," you respond, and then find yourself spending the next 20 minutes or more listening to a loosely and poorly-structured business plan coupled with less-than-realistic steps of implementation. You have just witnessed an example of those who have not prepared themselves for success; they are less-than-qualified borrowers with less-than-meaningful business plans. People who are smart prepare well ahead and prepare thoroughly. Those who are not so smart display their lack of intelligence through poor preparation coupled with a belief that they can cuckold others into thinking that they will be successful.

You are well advised to spend your time with the former and avoid the latter! One of our financial advisors expressed it well. "There are two ways to go broke in business: Don't spend enough time with the right people, or spend too much time with the wrong people. If you do either, you'll be gone in six months." My singer-songwriter friend, Larry Jon Wilson, said it even better in a song, "I still have a drink or two, but only with a chosen few."

Successful executive leaders build discernment and learn to associate with others who are authentic and genuine, but a stumbling block to avoid is associating only with those whose generational heritage is consistent with your own. Any organization will have in it people from different age groups, and one of the challenges executive leaders face is integrating the multi-generational perspectives of the people in the business with the organizational culture. Greg Hammill articulates the challenges of managing a multi-generational workforce in his magazine article entitled, "Mixing and Managing for Generations of Employees."

Hammill describes differences in individuals' perspective on leadership on the basis of their common generational experiences. He begins with the World War II work group—people born between 1922 and 1945. These individuals generally believe in a hierarchy and a direct command and control form of leadership. They are by their nature practical, dedicated and accustomed to hard work. Also known as the "Greatest Generation," they were raised in an era of American progress and economic growth that was highlighted by traditional families, safe schooling and a new world order in which the US was ascendant. This generation came of age during the post-depression, World War II era and was called upon to serve a cause greater than themselves. This highly social, but shrinking, generation of Americans is eager to contribute in groups and to leave a legacy of benefit to others. What they look for in leaders is respect for their efforts and personal, rather than public, recognition.

Baby Boomers, born between 1946 and 1964, are a driven, workaholic group and tend to focus on consensus and collegial relationships. This generation was the largest in American history, numbering more than 75 million, and was raised in an era of extreme optimism, opportunity and progress. Most Boomers grew up in two-parent households with safe schools and job security. This generation is characterized by a deep reaction against all forms of tradition – religious, familial, and cultural. They are credited with Rock 'n Roll and the mass entry into the workforce and social upheaval that accompanied desegregation. Boomers can also be a self-absorbed generation that demands from their leaders personal recognition and opportunities for fulfillment. As evidence of this, we can look at boomers' divorce rates, their quest to "never be old," and their hunger for personal wealth and materialistic gain.

The Gen X group, born between 1964 and 1980, is quite different from the Boomers, since they are marked by skepticism, self-reliance and interest in eliminating the task. They are more interested in eliminating a job than performing it. This is the smallest generation in modern history, numbering fewer than 50 million. Considered to be the most ignored and misunderstood generation, Gen X-ers are the first generation in American history that will not do better, financially, than the previous generation. They grew up in two-career families with rapid, rising divorce rates, downsizing, the dawning of the high-tech and the information age, and the introduction of the entertainment culture. They seek to counter the instability of their youth with a drive for work-life balance. Their slant on leadership embraces demonstrating competence, challenging others and asking why.

The Gen Y group, born between 1981 and 2000, is a hopeful, ambitious, goal-oriented group who are often motivated by achievement and pulling together. This generation has replaced the Baby Boomers as the largest generation in US history, at more than 100 million strong. They are the most diverse, educated, marketed to, medicated, and cared for generation in history. Divorced parents raised nearly half the group; 33 percent lived with a single parent, and nearly 75 percent had working mothers. They are characterized as impatient, with a high need for immediate response. They also reflect the shift to real-time information sharing. This generation spent their early years in an era of rapid American economic growth and prosperity and the presence of America as the lone superpower, but they were the first to lack the security of safe schools or stable home environments. The Gen Y group exhibit confidence, connectedness and values similar to the World War II group.

Future leaders will face the extraordinary challenge of managing the transition of power from the World War II generation, to the Baby Boomers, to the Gen X, to the Gen Y generations. Fortunately, as Hammill notes, all age groups share core values, especially the value of family, and all, regardless of age, want leaders they can trust.

My personal observations of cynicism and skepticism and plain laziness among a subset of workers of all generations spurred an interest in my learning more on the written history on the "seven deadly sins" of wrath, greed, sloth, pride, lust, envy and gluttony. I have been particularly intrigued by the observations of a variety of religious leaders, including the Christian monks, regarding the sin of sloth. Thomas Aquinas describes sloth as, "sadness and abhorrence or boredom regarding a spiritual and divine god." He refers to what happens when a person becomes incapable of being stimulated by anything good or beautiful or wise; or worse, when goodness, beauty or wisdom evoke a response of disgust or a cynical thought. When we lose the passion for life, goodness, laughter and joy, a challenge executive leaders face because of the seriousness of the issues they face as part of their job responsibilities, then it may be a sign that sloth has a grip on us.

In our current day, extremism may arise from sloth. My father was often asked later in his life if he was a conservative or a liberal. His response? "I am well educated and an intellectual–therefore I can't be anything but a moderate." It is wise to realize that you can easily offend others by being extreme as either a conservative or a liberal. If brought into conversations on politics, social, religious or economic issues, it is important to have facts and background information to support your opinions. Not knowing facts and information is not preferable, however; believing what "ain't so" is even worse. Humorist Will Rogers, who had a way of getting to the heart of a matter, stated in a conversation towards former FBI Director J. Edgar Hoover, "It's not what he doesn't know that bothers me. It's what he knows for sure that just ain't so."

Another of the real challenges in becoming an effective leader is the need to have influence. Author and sales consultant, Jeffrey Gitomer, puts it this way, "If you think a leader can lead with no authority, rethink that immediately." Imagine a person of great influence standing outside a major corporation, but not having a job in the company. Would you follow him or her? There is no single key to successful leadership, but you must have a combination of authority and influence. In my experience, you develop your position of authority primarily through your career, and secondly by your connections with power. Quite simply, authority gives leaders the ability to influence.

While building your authority and influence, you must also achieve professionalism. Great leaders are not only respected; they are also measured. They are routinely measured against their tasks and goals. You can avoid failing to reach your goals and accomplish your tasks by being steadfast in purpose.

You will not be alone in being measure against your work goals. In fact, all employees in your organization should be measured against their work goals. When goals are met, and especially when they are exceeded, it is important for you to celebrate victories. Most leaders enjoy celebrations and confirmations of success, and these celebrations confirm that the organization recognizes achievement, rather than focusing solely on punishing failure. Real leaders know how to create genuine celebrations and recognition of all who participated in the success. They also know how to temper celebration and to springboard it as a way to build momentum for the next task.

Another one of my mentors, the late Dr. Joe Greene, knew how to celebrate success and is worthy of being celebrated himself. As an African-American who grew up in rural Emanuel County, Georgia, Joe became an insurance executive, earned his Doctorate in Education (Ed.D.), became a highly-respected college professor, and served ably as chairman of the Board of Regents of the University System of Georgia. Joe's skills enabled him to hold many leadership positions, including serving as a valuable member of the Georgia-Carolina Bancshares and First Bank boards, as well as a number of board committee positions. He always impressed me with his very objective thinking and his life celebration towards virtually all accomplishments. Joe came a long way from the cotton fields of Emanuel County.

Like Joe Greene, everyone who aspires to an executive leadership position would do well to celebrate success and be willing to work to overcome the inevitable struggles along the way. Positive and proper vision, good planning and full communications, coupled with associating with good mentors, allow us to accept and manage our frustrations while meeting the great challenges that are not for the faint of heart. Even as you build your leadership capabilities within your organization, you will also want to build your ability to lead in the community and other extra-organizational settings, and the next chapter suggests how to do that effectively.

EXPANDING YOUR LEARNING TOWARDS GREATER LEADERSHIP OPPORTUNITIES

One of my bedrock beliefs is that leaders are called upon to contribute to the common good in their own organizations and in the community at large. Leading effectively in the volunteer world differs from leading effectively in your own for-profit organization, however, I have found very little written about what it takes to be an effective leader in the volunteer world. Therefore, in this chapter, we will discuss the considerations that will help you determine the cause to which you can contribute most and the manner in which you can do so.

Your first decision should be selecting causes or programs that are compatible with your lifestyle and in which you have a personal passion and perhaps a skill or talent. I have known symphony board members who appeared to have no knowledge of symphony music and could not distinguish Mozart from Puccini or Verdi from Wagner. Beyond a personal passion for your cause, you must consider whether you can commit fully to a board membership or leadership role. I learned from my father that experience, knowledge, commitment and adequate time to help others are some of the most important qualifications for able board members and leaders. It has been estimated that you should be prepared to serve up to a minimum of 35 days per year for *each* board on which you agree to serve.

Once you select causes about which you are passionate and determine that you can make a full commitment to board membership, you must assess your qualifications as a board member. One of your qualifications should be a high level of decision-making experience and personal knowledge of at least one of the following areas: public policy, service technology, communications, sales, finance, accounting, membership development, volunteerism, or legal guidelines.

Only select boards on which to serve that have a clear objective that will add significant value. I witnessed this in action when I was growing up as I observed my father organize dozens and dozens of special events for a diverse and wide range of purposes; charity, professional, and political. He always had a clear objective toward which all activities were directed and, at the end, a significant value was achieved. I was able to put these lessons into action when I began volunteering during high school and college days and learned the great pride that accompanies organizing special events, always with an objective and always with a value to achieve.

An important consideration when volunteering is the organization's ability to direct the vast majority of funds raised by the Board through its activities toward the cause involved, reserving only a small minority of funds for administrative and ongoing fundraising costs. To me, the most successful events are those that guarantee a high level of funding with virtually all start-up expenses raised in advance through sponsorships and contributions. Most volunteer leaders commit to using minimal funds for administration and fund-raising events, so that the majority of funds raised go to support the cause of the organization. For example, the Carter Center's 2011 annual report indicates that only 2.9% of their expenses are administrative costs and only 4.0% are for fundraising. In contrast, a 2012 report from the March of Dimes indicates that fully 24.2% of their contributions go toward administrative costs and fundraising. Those who contribute to the funding of an event or a sponsoring organization want to know that the organizers exercised prudent expense control. Those who purchase tickets or offer sponsorship for events want to know that their expenditures are used to add value, even as the event is meaningful, reasonable, and enjoyable for the attendees.

Excessive start-up expenses and excessive volunteerism are undesirable, especially when there is very little accomplished and virtually no financial gain for the non-profit organization. In other words, there is a finite limit to the personal and financial resources that any one individual or organization can devote to volunteer activities, therefore, organizational leaders should make a conscious choice to be involved in those volunteer activities that will not over-extend personal or organizational resources and that will result in a net gain for the non-profit in question. During late 2006, I was asked to serve as the upcoming Chairman of the 2007 Augusta regional Heart Ball. The planning and organizing period for the ball was during the holiday season leading up to the ball in February, but, fortunately, the Ball had a very well-organized committee of approximately twelve volunteers who functioned very well without supervision. As a result, the committee was able to begin its work even without meeting in person and to stage a most enjoyable Ball that netted in excess of $100,000 raised for the Georgia Heart Association.

While we were busy working on the Heart Association Ball, I observed one of our other neighborhood non-profits also organizing a community fundraising event. This other non-profit had an organizing committee of 37 individuals and 12 subcommittees! The group was successful in several areas; raising large sums of sponsorship from the business community, meeting frequently, planning feverishly, and pulling off a very expensive event. Unfortunately, the group was unsuccessful in accomplishing its main objective, since most of the funds raised were used to cover the cost of the event, with few dollars remaining to be given to the non-profit organization involved. While their event was well done, they missed a prime opportunity to add value to the organization for which the event took place. They added little value with their fundraising event.

One of the most meaningful of my board memberships is that of the Community Bankers Association of Georgia, whose bylaws require that all officers and directors of the Association must come from the executive officer ranks of their respective bank or banking company. It has been a special pleasure to serve on this board for the past 23 years. Board meetings are quarterly, and eventful, generally lasting one hour and including significant accomplishments. The CBA board meetings adhere to a high level of business protocol with board discussions based on reasonable, ethical, and fair deliberations.

The relationship between a CEO of the organization and the Board is based on reciprocal interdependence and is a true partnership. The CEO is a strong performer and the board functions with a full committee system made up of an executive committee, an audit committee, and a finance committee, with each committee independent of the others. The effective committee system is why a board needs to have at least 12-15 members to fulfill its independence. Other valuable committees may often include human resource, marketing, and strategic planning committees.

In comparison to the Community Bankers Association, during these same years I also served on a national, non-profit foundation board. When asked to serve, I assumed that this national board would be made up of corporate CEOs, CFOs and the like, but when I arrived at their headquarters for my first meeting, I found a very average group of people whose membership on the board was based strictly on their early connections to a common professional fraternal organization. The self-centered board members would arrive for the meeting in t-shirts and shorts, eat pizza, drink beer and discuss silly details for eight to ten hours straight! There was no structure or value to the meetings and little was contributed to the well-being of the foundation. It was apparent that the majority of these foundation board members had no mentors, no understanding of fundraising responsibilities, and were locked into simple minded and elementary middle-management thinking. Ironically, there was little leadership on this so-called leadership board of the foundation.

I have also served on a board and as Chairman of the board of another leadership organization that seemed to have a different perspective, relying primarily on staff members as volunteer board members and officers. During my years of service on the board, a 30-year anniversary event was planned and held with much success. This organization had recruited only three CEOs as their Chairpersons during their three decades of existence.

Just as it is critically important to build a relationship with a mentor in your professional career pursuits, it is also difficult to overstate the value of mentor relationships as you develop your ability to lead in your volunteer pursuits. In my opinion, this may be the most important element in the making of aspiring leaders. Mentoring creates learning experiences that enable you to build your big-picture thinking and objective fact-finding skills as components of effective decision making. Further, it supports highly ethical thinking and behavior that is consistent with and supports the mission of the organization.

Without question, my greatest influences throughout my career came from my working relationships with successful and highly ethical businessmen and businesswomen. My commitment to the formation of Georgia-Carolina Bancshares and the reorganization of First Bank originated from a Sunday afternoon meeting with leading businessmen J. Lee, George Inman, and Julian Osbon. I had known J. Lee for some time and considered him to be one of the most straightforward and ethical individuals that I knew. George Inman was someone I had known only through being part of the same community, but even from that vantage point, I knew him to be a man of honor and someone I considered a hero or mentor. Julian Osbon was a future-thinking businessman I had always considered one of my favorite friends. I was not looking for a new career opportunity, but I was very impressed by their coming together for a new business venture, a new commercial bank for Metro Augusta, Georgia. They represented an extended group of successful businessmen who formed an alliance with a group of business men and women from Thomson, Georgia, and launched Augusta's Georgia-Carolina-First Bank banking franchise. I was honored to be asked to serve as President of the new banking company and to be mentored by these fine business leaders and am pleased that, through our collaborative efforts, the resulting organization has been one of the most successful and respected bank organizations in Georgia.

My late mentor, Georgia Banking commissioner E. D. "Jack" Dunn, would often suggest that, "a bank board of directors should be a gentlemen's club," later amended to, "a ladies' and gentlemen's club." He would go on to say that "there should never be a shootout at the board table." The influence of my mentors and, perhaps, a bit of the luck o' the Irish enabled me to have 34 years of good results in performance and 34 years of friendly, upbeat Annual Meetings—with no shootouts! Further, due to excellent mentoring and good board choices, most of my boards were also ladies' and gentlemen's clubs. In part, I believe I obtained these results because I learned how to select and work with good Board members, and in the next chapter I will share these lessons with you.

UNDERSTANDING GOOD GOVERNANCE: THE ROLE OF THE BOARD OF DIRECTORS

One of the major responsibilities of executive leaders is providing solid and transparent governance for the organization. It is critical for leaders to fully understand the protocols of both the corporate and the non-profit world. Therefore, one of the important keys to providing good leadership is to have a complete working knowledge of good governance, which strengthens the organization by providing critical capital, intellect, reputation, resources, and access to power for profit or non-profit success. The ultimate in good governance comes from building a constructive partnership between the chief executive of the non-profit organization and the Board, based on the recognition that the effectiveness of the organization and the effectiveness of the board are interdependent. The board cannot govern well without the chief executive's collaboration, and the chief executive cannot lead the organization to its full potential without the board's unflagging support. While respecting the organizational model, exceptional boards become allies with the chief executive in pursuit of the mission. The recognition of this interdependence is often foolishly overlooked by political boards, public councils and political commissions.

Exceptional boards, in cooperation with their chief executives, create an environment based on respect and candor that fosters a productive exchange of views. They are not afraid to question each other or to challenge management. A culture that invites questions requires trust that is built upon experience with fellow board members. Exceptional boards value personal relationships in a team setting and create opportunities for interactions among boards and executive staff members. There is also a democratic process, or an element of cultural inquiry, that is the responsibility of non-profit boards. They cultivate and distribute leadership across the board, rather than concentrating it in a handful of officers or an executive committee, so that the organization is not dependent upon just a few select individuals.

Boards have primary legal and fiduciary responsibility for governance – the exercise and assignment of power and authority in their organizations. They reserve to themselves organizational oversight and the role of policy setting and delegate to the chief executive the responsibility for managing operations and resources. Exceptional boards should not just be outside examiners, but should also be powerful forces supporting the organization and its chief executive and staff.

The board's first duty is describing why the organization exists and what it hopes to accomplish. One of the most important roles of a non-profit board is to set the organization's course, to provide direction, and to look for horizons in terms of years, not months. Exceptional boards and board members also understand their accountability to the community and constituents' needs and give voice to the enduring values, stories and aspirations that shape the organization. It is important to note from a leadership perspective that one must take community and constituent needs into account while making decisions. What's important to the community and constituents should be of paramount interest to the organization and board.

Exceptional boards then translate these elements into a compelling articulation of mission, vision and core values that guide major decisions and everyday activities. They affirm the organization's mission, chart a future course and define priorities. Most non-profits tend to conduct a strategic planning event every three to five years. Many place the strategic report, when complete, on a shelf and never discuss the planning event again for another three to five years. Exceptional boards treat questions of mission, vision, and core values not as exercises to be done once, but as statements of crucial importance to be embraced and developed into all deliberations. Effective for profit and non-profit boards use the strategic plan to establish financial and program goals. Many also use the plan to assess the performance of the CEO and staff. They also use it to drive meeting agendas and to shape board recruitment. With the involvement of the CEO and staff, exceptional boards develop, protect, and advance a clear mission that they use as a platform for advocacy, fundraising, grant making for non-profits and marketing. In brief, exceptional boards translate strategic priorities into action plans for themselves.

It is natural for the vision to bring the mission to life. The vision should also carry the board and the CEO in the direction the organization is going. Strategic thinking derives from and drives strategic planning. Exceptional boards are active partners with the CEO and staff in framing and assessing the strategic plan. Exceptional boards do not relegate strategic thinking to a periodic exercise; rather they make it an ongoing, regular part of the board's work and the board's meeting agendas.

An organization which has charitable status creates a special obligation to the organization's beneficiaries and the public for a non-profit board. Government regulations, watchdog agencies and the media play an active role in shaping public perception. Exceptional boards ensure that the public has access to clear, accurate and timely information that enables a valid determination of whether the organization is using its tax-exempt status appropriately. Boards make sure that the organization posts its IRS form 990 or 990-PF on the organization's website and offers unencumbered access to audited financial statements and reports of programmatic accomplishments. These boards understand that it is in the best interest of the organization to develop open relationships with staff and donors, as well as stakeholders and the community at large. Working with staff, exceptional boards ensure that donors are treated with respect, receive forthright reports on the use of their funds and are advised of notable developments. At the same time, they distinguish between the need for transparency and the importance of confidentiality. Exceptional boards ensure that transparency is extended internally. They receive information of significance and every board member has equal access to relevant materials when making decisions. Selecting people to be Board members, therefore, is a very important task and one that will be the topic of discussion in the next chapter.

ENACTING GOOD GOVERNANCE: SELECTING THE BEST BOARD MEMBERS

Once you are certain that you understand the appropriate role for a Board of Directors, the next challenge is selecting appropriate and effective individuals to serve on the board. I have experienced board behavior that was virtually dysfunctional due to the lack of appropriate board talent. The many examples of dysfunctional boards that I have witnessed lead me to believe that it is important, first of all, to understand who might be *in*appropriate as a board member before learning the science of building strong and effective boards. Keep in mind that these recommendations are not pronouncements about the character of these groups of potential Board members, but are general guidelines regarding background and occupational characteristics that contribute the most to the Board fulfillments and the success of the organization.

Retired executives may, upon initial consideration, seem to be perfect candidates for board membership, given their experience of making decisions from a top-level perspective. However, while retired executives can be helpful as consultants, it is important to understand that most of these people have already contributed untold hours of service in volunteer roles throughout their careers. Thus, they should be approached only with the understanding that they should enjoy the freedom of choosing their own level of volunteerism in their retirement years. There is a long list of retired executives with whom I have lunch at least annually. These luncheons are planned as a special treat for all and as a gesture of thanks for past services, with no official business to be discussed.

Another group that should seldom be selected for board membership is people who are currently in middle management positions. Very often, people in middle management do not have the inclination or experience to take a strategic, top-level perspective of an organization. Effective boards need men and women whose experience and inclinations steer them toward thinking about the organization from a holistic perspective. People who are mid-level managers are unlikely to have had significant experience making the most difficult of decisions, and may therefore be incapable of exercising the thought processes required to make difficult decisions or having the backbone to implement them. Unfortunately, because their salaries and bonuses are not commensurate with those of an effective CEO, middle managers may not have an accurate perspective of effective leadership compensation.

Professional fundraisers are another group who are generally inappropriate members of non-profit boards. One of the jobs of a non-profit board is procuring financial support and fundraising, therefore, professional fundraisers may experience a conflict of interest between their career and their board responsibilities. One of my best advisors made the dramatic statement that all successful residential real estate salespeople must naturally hate each other at the end of the day, and surely this must be true of people in other careers, such as professional fundraisers.

I would also suggest that those who "feed at the public trough" by holding governmental or quasi-governmental positions may not be good board candidates. Public officials are certainly laudable for their willingness to devote their careers to public service, but they generally do not serve well on corporate and non-profit boards. Natural conflicts result from their need to address their own public agendas and to avoid interpersonal conflicts. A strong committed board member must have a deep positive commitment to the mission and agenda of the organization on whose board they serve. Regretfully, there are many occasions when public officials do not have the unquestionable reputation that should belong to a valid for-profit or non-profit board member.

It is never a good idea to enlist board members who are each other's competitors in their careers. During my experiences of offering support to good causes, I hope I have been cooperative with my competition for the betterment of the community, however, I have never felt the need to aid my competitors in fulfilling their missions or their personal goals. You will <u>never</u> see me playing golf, having dinner, or even having a social beverage with a competitor. One of the most inappropriate suggestions I have received from a non-profit executive was a glib question, "why don't you banks get together and sponsor our reception?" If we were willing to follow such a foolish suggestion, the collective efforts would totally discount any real public relations value. It is to everyone's benefit, as well as much more meaningful, for organizations like banks to choose their sponsorships individually and separate from their competitor's interests.

I have a very high and appropriate regard for members of the clergy and have had a number of interesting experiences in organizational behavior with friends who are people of the cloth. Early on, I thought that the official first course of any seminary education program must surely be Fundraising 101, since clergy members so often "pass the hat," but my first observations of board members who were career clergy was that they were not comfortable soliciting contributions.Members of the clergy also seem to be uncomfortable making tough decisions, which is understandable. Leadership on a board requires fundraising and a certain number of hard decisions, therefore, I do not recommend selecting clergy persons as board members. There are important occasions, however, when organizations need a chaplain and/or a spiritual advisor.

Although many educators have leadership skills, they often do not enjoy fundraising, nor do they have the strong influential contacts needed to serve as a competent fundraiser or board leader. Over the years, I have seen educators make attempts to serve as president or chairman of an active non-profit; however this is often difficult without adequate resources, funds, staff support and general corporate assets. Educators can, however, serve as valid advisors.

"Worker bees" should remain as worker bees and should not be considered board material. I have seen many errors made through attempts to elevate "worker bees" to board or officer positions. Worker bees generally have a mentality very much like middle managers. They are accustomed to being task oriented and to working on mundane activities, but are not comfortable with making tough decisions based on the big picture issues of corporate responsibilities.

In every community there are individuals who are compulsive volunteers. These individuals seem to think they are capable of serving on every volunteer board in the community, but the reality is that they often become over committed with the result that all of their efforts become ineffective. These compulsive volunteers often do not understand the competitive nature of community service and the necessity for fundraising among non-profit groups. While these individuals are typically confident in their leadership skills, their confidence often seems misplaced. In fact, I often see these volunteers actually creating problems for the executive directors and the traditional board members. Volunteers should select those causes, such as feeding the hungry, historic preservation, symphonic music, public education and the military, with which they possess a deep identification. A good community leader simply can't be all things to all causes.

While settling into many of my leadership roles on Boards of Directors, I have often been advised that as the new Chairman I would have the privilege of appointing multiple new members to the board and asked whether I would like to use The List as an aid in my selection process. The first time this occurred, assuming that The List was something with which I should be familiar, I considered and rejected a variety of lists that came to mind (surely not "Best Dressed"!?), finally concluding that I should select the safe route and ask, "What list?" The answer: "The list of those who have an interest in serving on this board!" You may think it sounds strange, but my response was, "Why would I want to see The List?" Shouldn't our goal be to choose the very best leaders to serve on our boards, rather than limiting our choices to those who have expressed an interest in board positions? We have considered some groups of people who are typically not good Board members. Our next challenge, then, is to discover how best to identify and select those who will be the very best leaders for our boards.

First and foremost, the very best choices for a public *or* private board of directors should always be men and women with a high degree of prudence and diligence, two very different characteristics. A prudent director is one who embraces common sense, practical wisdom and informed judgment. Diligence requires effort and attention to duty. The duty of an officer of an organization is more concerned with the day-to-day operations, whereas the director's duty is essentially one of oversight. The duty of diligence requires certain basic actions, including attending meetings on a regular basis, preparing for meetings by reviewing information concerning the action to be taken by the board, and general oversight of the board's activities. The actions of the directors undertaken in good faith and for a rational business purpose will ordinarily be protected by their business judgment. Directors of corporations discharge their fiduciary duties when, in good faith, they exercise business judgment in making decisions regarding the corporation.

In choosing directors, a committee and/or organization should also look for people who are moving into leadership positions, such as the CEO position of their companies. Candidates should have the personal skills of making decisions on a big-picture level and should always exercise ethical judgment in their service to the corporation. While drawing from the best of the community, there may well be an appropriate CEO of a local marketing firm that can offer quality guidance on marketing and public relations issues. The bylaws of the Community Bankers Association of Georgia call for all officers and directors of the association to be executive officers of member banks. This board has proven to be one of the most effective boards on which I have served, at least partially because of this selection criterion.

Since the passage of the Sarbanes-Oxley (SOX) Act, there has been an interest in strengthening the role of audit committees of both for-profit and not-for-profit organizations. As a result, having an accounting expert on the Audit Committee and the board will aid the organization in understanding complex accounting and financial control decisions. With the new SOX requirements, it is extremely helpful to have a member of the board who is a public-spirited CPA. It is also helpful to have other members of the board who have experience in accounting or finance. Boards benefit by having a public-spirited attorney on the board as well.

Many communities are fortunate enough to have senior retired military officers in their midst. My community of Augusta, Georgia has been quite successful in bringing these retired officers into active community life.

In general, the board should represent the best-of-the-best in your community to enable you to be successful in promoting and telling your story effectively. Identify the best community leaders by looking at public surveys where the results list the most powerful leaders and the biggest givers. These surveys will also confirm those who are not leaders. Leaders on your board should represent a family or group that is highly regarded in the community that they serve. They should be individuals without conflicts of interest in their service because this is the right thing to do, and because most boards today have their board members read and sign Conflict of Interest statements. The final step in confirming the viability of a potential board member is to ensure that they have the time, personal funds, and resources available to fully support the mission of the organization.

At the time that King Edward III claimed the French throne in 1344, he founded the oldest and most prestigious order of chivalry in the United Kingdom. The Most Noble Order of the Garter was dedicated to the image and arms of Saint George as England's patron saint. It is anticipated that the Normans learned and embraced some of their virtues from the Romans. In particular, the Noble Order only considered new members from families with three consecutive generations of known dignity and honor. This three consecutive generation requirement discounted the marginal consideration of the noveau riche that lack political and cultural sophistication.

LEADERSHIP AND THE COURAGEOUS FOLLOWER

"Know thyself."

-The Oracle at Delphi

In the process of coming to know yourself, you may decide that executive leadership is not the path you wish to take and that being a follower is a better path for you. Even if you do take the road to executive leadership, you will not be the leader in every situation. There will be times when the appropriate role for you is that of the follower. Clearly, without followers, there would be no leadership. Thinking of leaders without followers is akin to thinking of teachers without students—neither makes sense because leadership and followership are two parts of one whole, and successful leaders recognize their reciprocal interdependence with followers. The role of followers is critical to the role of leaders. Successful leaders, regardless of the profession, industry, or culture hold their followers in high esteem and view the development of followers as a critical part of their executive leadership responsibilities. In this chapter, we explore the connections between leaders and followers, the responsibility leaders have for followers, and the responsibility that followers have in their roles.

"Followers" is not a synonym for subordinates. A subordinate reports to an individual of higher rank in an organization and might, in practice, be a supporter, an antagonist, or indifferent about the organization. A follower is someone who shares a common purpose with a leader, believes in what the organization is trying to accomplish, wants both the leader and the organization to succeed, and works energetically to that end. Leaders build strong relationships with followers through the attitudes they hold about followers and their behaviors toward followers.

Successful leaders have high expectations of themselves and others, especially their followers. Just as successful leaders strive to be their best, they expect their followers to do the same. The goal of these leaders is not to create a group of mirror images of themselves, but rather to help others achieve their full potential. Successful leaders' ability to visualize the skills and attitudes that are necessary for success enables them to be a positive influence on others by encouraging others to build their skills and attitudes as a way to achieve their own success at reaching their goals.

Successful leaders believe that growth is a journey, not a destination. Even though team members may be satisfied with their present position or current level of responsibility within the company, winning leaders do not allow this to prevent them from growing. Instead, leaders implement programs and incentives and invent new ways for people to continue to grow, expand and improve, even if they stay in their current position.

Successful leaders practice what they preach. Successful leaders set a good example for others both on and off the job. They demonstrate integrity by being transparent examples for others through their consistency between words and deeds. My father was an example of this type of leader, often referred to today as a "transformational" leader, who takes joy in their work because they recognize the importance of doing one's best while simultaneously valuing strong positive relationships with others. Leaders such as these are believable role models and command respect from others. I believe that this is one of the main reasons my father received so much appreciation for his work.

Successful leaders coach others. One of the most important characteristics of successful leaders is their focus beyond themselves. They serve as mentors to others, demonstrating their desire to help others reach their goals. Leaders are patient and encouraging, and frequently coach others by educating, counseling and demonstrating through their own behaviors. I have mentioned repeatedly the importance of my mentors in helping me understand not only how to be an executive leader, but also how to lead a good life.

Successful leaders teach other team members to become coaches. Successful leaders teach others to stretch and share their own skills by becoming coaches to others. Everyone should have the opportunity to become a coach to at least one member of your organization's team. By teaching team members to coach one another, you can create a powerful chain of successful leadership within your organization.

Successful leaders track performance. Successful leaders create a definable standard of performance against which everything is measured. They make the standards of performance, along with their expectations, clear so that followers know what they are expected to do and at what level they are expected to perform. Leaders' standards are customized to each member of the team, allowing them to give responsibility, as well as expect accountability.

Successful leaders know that practice makes perfect. Great leaders understand that the only way they and their followers can maintain a high level of achievement is through repetition and discipline. By practicing the previously-mentioned secrets of success, leaders' daily actions become habits that form the basis of their continued success. Likewise, becoming a courageous follower, like becoming a good human being, is both a daily and lifelong task.

Successful leaders listen to followers. Effective leaders have a responsibility to support the conditions of courageous followership and to respond productively to acts of courageous followers. When this is done, it offers powerful paybacks to the leader, the followers, and the organization and demonstrates the leaders' belief in followers.

Successful leaders know how to follow. Even the most successful and highranking leaders are not in a leadership position at all times in their life; most of us are leaders in some situations and followers in others. Ira Chaleff, author of *The Courageous Follower*, acknowledges that, because ego strength is one of the qualities that propels people into leadership positions, it may be difficult for leaders, as it is for society in general, to appreciate the importance of followers. Following is sometimes viewed with disdain, due to the image of following as docility, conformity, weakness, and failure to succeed. This image could not be further from reality when we consider the power held by followers and the virtues of having powerful followers supporting powerful leaders.

Courageous followership is built on the platform of courageous relationships, including the courage to be right, the courage to be wrong, and the courage to be different from each other. All executive leaders *must* understand that each of us sees the world through our own eyes and experiences, therefore, our interpretation of the world will be unique. Among the many things we learn from relationships, is the value of maintaining the validity of our own interpretations of the world while learning to respect the validity of others' interpretations.

In his book about followers, Chaleff suggests there are five dimensions of courageous followership:

1. The courage to assume responsibility. Courageous followers assume responsibility for themselves and the organizations they serve.

2. The courage to serve. Courageous followers are not afraid of the hard work required to serve as followers.

3. The courage to challenge. Courageous followers give voice to the discomfort they feel when either the behaviors or

policies of the leader or of the group conflict with their own sense of right and wrong.

4. The courage to participate in transformation. When behavior that jeopardizes the common purpose remains unchanged, courageous followers recognize the need for transformation.

5. The courage to take moral action. Courageous followers know when it is time to take a stand that is different from that of the leaders. In this sense, they are answering to a higher set of values, an action that may involve personal risk, but service to the common purpose justifies and sometimes demands our actions.

In Chaleffs writings on *The Courageous Follower*, he offers the following meditation as a guide toward becoming a good follower. We end this chapter with his meditation and the thought that it might be a meditation that is relevant for a large number of situations in life, not just followership.

- I am a steward of this group and share responsibility for its success;
- I am responsible for adhering to the highest value I can envision;
- I am responsible for my successes and failures and for conformity to learn from them;
- I am responsible for the attractive and unattractive parts of who I am;
- I can empathize with others who are also important;
- As an adult, I can relate on a peer basis to other adults who are the group's formal leaders;

- I can support leaders and counsel them, and receive counsel and support from them;
- Our common purpose is our best guide;
- I have the power to help leaders use their power wisely and effectively;
- If leaders abuse power, I can learn from others and change my behavior;
- If abusive leaders do not change their behavior, I can and will withdraw my support;
- By staying true to my values, I can serve others well and fulfill my potential;
- Thousands of courageous acts by followers, can, one by one, improve the world;
- Courage always exists in the present, what can I do today?

LA DOLCE VITA:
THE LEGACY WE LEAVE

"Those who have torches shall pass them on to others."   —Plato

Although the phrase "to give back" is so overused as to make it a cliché, I do believe in the biblical phrase, "For unto whomsoever much is given, of him [or her] shall be much required; and to whom him have committed much, of him they will ask for more." Those of us who have the privilege of leading others have certainly been given much, therefore we bear a special responsibility to contribute to the well-being of people in our communities and beyond by striving to attend to the needs of those who are marginalized by society, to endeavor to eradicate that societal marginalization thus building a healthier society, and to walk softly upon the Earth and its resources.

My maternal grandfather, G. B. (Jake) Pollard, Sr., was considered the political boss of Columbia County, Georgia during his time, but, far from the stereotyped corrupt southern political boss, he was a humble, kind-hearted gentleman who was a true servant leader. His advice to one and all that, "if you can't help folks, you should get out of the courthouse," was a testament to his servant leader's heart. Grandfather Pollard often advised my brothers and me that we should always reach out to others with compassion and understanding and that we should never allow the other party in a business transaction or debate to be larger than we were in compassion, understanding, or willingness to find compromise or make amends.

Unfortunately, far too many examples exist in current times of poor leadership evidenced by unethical behavior and incivility. Has there ever been a time where what passes for public discourse has been so mean-spirited, bitter and unreasonable? Has there ever been a time where so many previously venerable Wall Street institutions collapsed as a result of treating unethical practices and greed as normal behavior and, further, undergirding these behaviors with a system of rules and regulations that protect institutions rather than individual investors? Have we ever seen so many people going unpunished, despite defrauding millions of investors of their lifetime savings? These examples illustrate a total rejection of the notion that we should consider the common good and how our actions affect others. Instead, the notion seems to be that if we all behave as selfish individuals, producing little and consuming much, somehow all will be well.

In contrast to this perspective, my belief that a basic law of our world is that the strong should have an interest in the needs of the weak, and this leads me to conclude that the key to life is to accomplish things that are good for someone or something larger than you. To truly serve as leaders, we must first dedicate ourselves to learning and fully understanding the concepts of altruism and benevolence. For, until we genuinely share a charitable interest in others, we greatly reduce our potential to lead. Under the banner of civility, we need to be a nation of citizens and business men and women who care about the common good, and those who have the most to contribute should lead the way. We need to give through our interactions with people in our daily lives, and we need to give through what we accomplish. This is the ultimate path to the "sweet life."

My hope is that this book will enlarge your opportunities to contribute to a cause larger than yourself by showing you how to understand and navigate the nuances of executive leadership. You have seen in this book that leadership, which is evident even in the laws of nature, may arise from innate skill, from learning, and from exigencies that force you into a leadership position. In any of these paths to leadership, you must assess your own leadership possibilities, measured against the best traits of leaders, and use that information to chart your unique path as a leader. Your self-exploration may lead you to conclude that followership is a more reasonable alternative for you, but should you continue on the journey toward executive leadership, be sure to take the critically important step of finding mentors to help you on your way. Make a few important stops on your journey to develop your cultural literacy, and learn about organizational governance and proper organizational protocol. Be assured that you will encounter roadblocks and detours as you move up the organizational hierarchy and that you will experience the unique frustrations associated with serving as a leader.

My own business success, attributable in part to the luck o' the Irish, has more likely been due to my firm belief that if you treat people with respect, tell them the truth and try your best to do the right thing by them, they will respond with effort, loyalty, productivity and accomplishment far beyond the bounds of what we think of as normal. I truly believe that most people want to accomplish something great – something they can be proud of. I believe this is all quite normal.

We are a culture of great accomplishments in business, but that is not enough. The late college football coach, Erk Russell, summed it up in his two-word motto, "Do Right." There is so much to learn and understand about the nuances of executive leadership, but there is also the ultimate reward from being a servant leader. This is the path to *la dolce vita*. As King Solomon stated, "And also every man [and woman] should eat and drink, and enjoy the good of all his labor."

I wish you...

La Dolce Vita
And
Joie de Vivre

A LIST OF MY HEROES

Willie Ashbrook

Congressman Doug Barnard, Jr.

Chef Jim Beck

Avys Billue

John Pierce Blanchard, Sr.

James H. Blanchard

Judge Jim Blanchard, Jr.

Ken Blanchard

Dr. Pierce Gordon Blanchard

Russell A. Blanchard

Paul Brewer

Major General Douglas Buchholz

Libby Byus

Dr. Lee Ann Caldwell

Dr. Ed Cashin

Frank Christian

U. S. Senator Max Cleland

Kelvin Collins

D. Hugh Connolly

Sherman Drawdy

Ed Dunbar

Commissioner Jack Dunn

Ed Eckles

Rich Everitt

Dr. Joe Ezell

Durwood Fincher

Michael Firmin

Brigadier General Jeff Foley, Ret.

Dr. Carl Gooding

Dr. Joseph Greene

Ron Harrison

Julian Hester

Jay M. Jaffe

Patrick Keenan

Levings W. Laney

Joe McGlamery

Nancy McJunkin

U. S. Senator Sam Nunn

Olin Plunkett

G. B. "Jake" Pollard, Sr.

Coach Erk Russell

Michael Ryan

Governor Carl E. Sanders

Dr. Alex Sheshunoff

Major General Perry Smith, Ret.

Chef Heinz Sowinski

Ed Turner

Sheriff Charles Webster

Barney B. Whitaker

Joe Willis

Larry Jon Wilson

BIBLIOGRAPHY

AAA Diamond Ratings. *AAA Tour Book Guide*. Heathrow, Florida, AAA Publishing, 1937.

Bauerlein, Mark, Dr. *The Dumbest Generation*. New York, New York. Penguin Group, 2008.

Brantley, John. *Kids, Politics, and Teaching Them to Think*. Danielsville, Georgia, TTB Comunications, Inc., 2008.

Brillat-Savarin, Jean Anthelme. *The Physiology of Taste or Meditations on Transcendental Gastronomy*. Paris, France, Ourrage Theorique, 1826.

Brown, Lance. *Will Rogers Now! Conversations With*. Chicago, Illinois, 2008.

Buchholz, General Douglas. Conversations with. Fort Gordon, Georgia, 1994-2003.

Chaleff, Ira. *The Courageous Follower*. San Francisco, California, Banett-Koehler Publishers, Inc., 2009.

Christian, Frank. Conversations with. Augusta, Georgia, 2011.

Curator, Will Rogers Museum. Conversations with. Claremore, Oklahoma, 2008-2011.

Danziger, Danny and Gillingham, John. *1215 The Year of Magna Carta*. New York, New York, Simon & Schuster, 2005.

Darwin, Charles. *The Origin of Species*. New York, New York, Random House, Inc., 1859.

Davis, James C. *The Human Story*. New York, New York, Harper Collins Publishers, 2004.

Drawdy, Sherman. Conversations with. Augusta, Georgia, 1964-1973.

Dunaway, Felton, Conversations with. Augusta, Georgia, 1974-1976.

Gitomer, Jeffrey. *Many Elements Give Leaders Ability to Influence,* The Augusta Chronicle. Augusta, Georgia, August 22, 2010.

Hammill, Greg. *Mixing and Management for Generations of Employees*. FDU Magazine Online Winter/Spring, 2005.

Hirsch, E. D., Jr. *Cultural Literacy*. New York, New York, Random House, Inc., 1987.

King Solomon. *Ecclesiastes, New Believers Bible*. Riverside, California, Tyndale Publishers, Inc., 1996.

Korda, Michael. *Power: How to Obtain It, How To Use It*. New York, New York, Random House, Inc., 1969.

McCartney, William W. Quote, Investment Consultant. Augusta, Georgia, Email, 2008.

Apostle Paul. *Second Letter to the Corinthians, New Believers Bible*. Riverside, California, Tyndale House Publishers, Inc., 1996.

Plunkett, Olin. Conversations with. 1974-2012.

Roberts, Henry M. III, Evans, William, Jr. , Hanemann, Daniel H., and Balch, Thomas J. *Robert's Rules of Order Newly Revised.* Cambridge, Massachusetts, Persons Books Group, 1876-2000.

Shakespeare, William. *The Twelfth Night.* London, England, Isaac Taggard and Edward Blount, 1623.

Church of England, *Common Book of Prayer. Deadly Sins.* London, England, 1662.

The Source. *Twelve Principles of Governance That Power Exceptional Boards.* Published by Board Source, Washington, DC, 2008.

Tomlin, Graham, *The Seven Deadly Sins.* Oxford, England, Wilkinson House, 2007.

Tyndale House Foundation. *New Believers Bible.* Riverside, California, Tyndale House Publishers, Inc., 1996.

Whitaker, Barney B. Conversations with. Augusta, Georgia, 1967-1970.

Wilson, E. O. *Sociobiology.* Cambridge, Massachusetts, Harvard University Press, 2000.

Wilson, Larry Jon. Conversations with. Augusta, Georgia, 1990-2010.

Yasko-Mangum, Jamie L. Look, *Speak & Behave for Men.* New York, New York, Skyhorse Publishing, 2007.

Made in the USA
Middletown, DE
27 December 2015